D1556187

GREAT MYSTERIES

UFOs

OPPOSING VIEWPOINTS®

Look for these and other exciting *Great Mysteries: Opposing Viewpoints* books:

Amelia Earhart *by Jane Leder*
Anastasia, Czarina or Fake?
by Leslie McGuire
Animal Communication *by Jacci Cole*
The Assassination of President Kennedy
by Jeffrey Waggoner
Atlantis *by Wendy Stein*
The Beginning of Language
by Clarice Swisher
The Bermuda Triangle *by Norma Gaffron*
Bigfoot *by Norma Gaffron*
Dinosaurs *by Peter & Connie Roop*
The Discovery of America
by Renardo Barden
ESP *by Michael Arvey*
The Loch Ness Monster *by Robert San Souci*
Noah's Ark *by Patricia Kite*
Pearl Harbor *by Deborah Bachrach*
Poltergeists *by Peter & Connie Roop*
Pyramids *by Barbara Mitchell*
Reincarnation *by Michael Arvey*
The Shroud of Turin *by Daniel C. Scavone*
The Solar System *by Peter & Connie Roop*
Stonehenge *by Peter & Connie Roop*
The Trojan War *by Gail Stewart*
UFOs *by Michael Arvey*
Unicorns *by Norma Gaffron*
Witches *by Bryna Stevens*

GREAT MYSTERIES

UFOs

OPPOSING VIEWPOINTS®

by Michael Arvey

Greenhaven Press, Inc. P.O. Box 289009, San Diego, California 92128-9009

No part of this book may be reproduced or used in any form or by any means, electronic, mechanical, or otherwise, including but not limited to photocopy, recording, or any information storage and retrieval system, without prior written permission from the publisher.

Library of Congress Cataloging-in-Publication Data

Arvey, Michael, 1948-
UFOs.

(Great mysteries : opposing viewpoints)
Bibliography: p.
Includes index.
Summary: Presents opposing views of experts on ancient and modern-day reports of mysterious flying objects, and includes eyewitness descriptions of aliens and their kidnapping of human beings.
1. Unidentified flying objects—Juvenile literature.
[1. Unidentified flying objects] I. Title. II. Series:
Great mysteries (Saint Paul, Minn.)
TL789.A725 1989 001.9′42 89-11645
ISBN 0-89908-060-X

© Copyright 1989 by Greenhaven Press, Inc.
Every effort has been made to trace owners of copyright material.

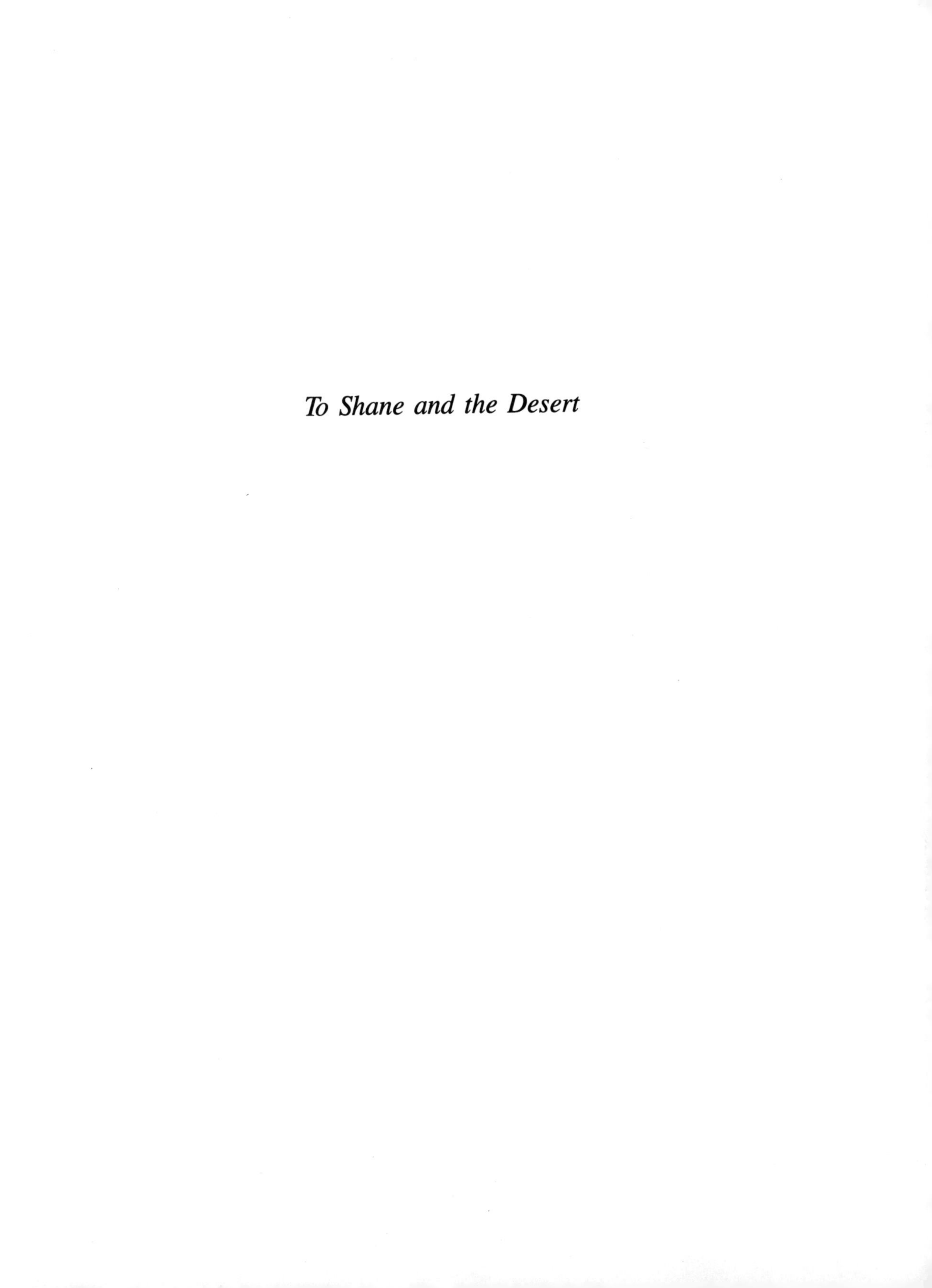

To Shane and the Desert

Contents

	Introduction	7
Prologue	Mysterious Objects in the Sky	8
One	Is There Life in Space?	14
Two	Did Extraterrestrials Visit Earth in Ancient Times?	30
Three	How Are UFOs Explained?	48
Four	Have UFOs Really Kidnapped People?	78
Five	Are Extraterrestrials Among Us?	94
Epilogue	The Mystery Continues	104
Appendix	Organizations to Contact	106
	About the Author	106
	For Further Exploration	107
	Additional Bibliography	108
	Index	110
	Picture Credits	112

Introduction

This book is written for the curious—those who want to explore the mysteries that are everywhere. To be human is to be constantly surrounded by wonderment. How do birds fly? Are ghosts real? Can animals and people communicate? Was King Arthur a real person or a myth? Why did Amelia Earhart disappear? Did history really happen the way we think it did? Where did the world come from? Where is it going?

Great Mysteries: Opposing Viewpoints books are intended to offer the reader an opportunity to explore some of the many mysteries that both trouble and intrigue us. For the span of each book, we want the reader to feel that he or she is a scientist investigating the extinction of the dinosaurs, an archaeologist searching for clues to the origin of the great Egyptian pyramids, a psychic detective testing the existence of ESP.

One thing all mysteries have in common is that there is no ready answer. Often there are *many* answers but none on which even the majority of authorities agrees. *Great Mysteries: Opposing Viewpoints* books introduce the intriguing views of the experts, allowing the reader to participate in their explorations, their theories, and their disagreements as they try to explain the mysteries of our world.

But most readers won't want to stop here. These *Great Mysteries: Opposing Viewpoints* aim to stimulate the reader's curiosity. Although truth is often impossible to discover, the search is fascinating. It is up to the reader to examine the evidence, to decide whether the answer is there—or to explore further.

"Penetrating so many secrets, we cease to believe in the unknowable. But there it sits nevertheless, calmly licking its chops."

H.L. Mencken, American essayist

Prologue

Mysterious Objects in the Sky

Perhaps you have seen the movie *Close Encounters of the Third Kind* or *E.T.* Perhaps you are a Trekkie—someone who is a fan of the television series ''Star Trek.'' Perhaps you have watched ''Flash Gordon'' or ''Buck Rogers.'' And perhaps you have at some time read in a book, a magazine, or a newspaper, reports such as this one that appeared in *Extra-Terrestrials Among Us,* a book by UFO writer George C. Andrews.

> The city of Gorki is strictly off-limits to anyone without a special Soviet government pass. . . . On March 27, 1983, a cigar-shaped UFO [unidentified flying object] about the size of a Boeing 747 hovered over Gorki Airport at low altitude for about 40 minutes. No jets were scrambled. After 40 minutes, it disappeared over the horizon without incident.

Another report in the same book stated:

> Approximately 200 British and American military and civilian personnel witnessed a UFO landing near a base which the U.S. Air Force shares with the Royal Air Force at Woodridge in Suffolk, at 3 a.m. on December 27, 1980. Among them was USAF Lieutenant Colonel Charles Halt, the Deputy Commander of the 81st Tactical Fighter Wing, which is stationed beside the RAF at Woodridge. He filed a report on

This UFO was photographed in British Columbia, Canada, by Hannah McRoberts in October 1981. She was photographing the mountains and neither she nor her companions saw the UFO at the time.

"Of course the flying saucers are real—and they are interplanetary."

British Air Chief Marshal Lord Dowding, *Reuters*, 1954

"The idea of wondrous spaceships from a distant civilization really is a fairy story."

UFO investigator and skeptic Philip Klass, *UFOs Explained*

the incident, which was intended to remain confidential. However, a copy of it, bearing his signature, reached the London weekly *News of the World*, which ran the story on October 2, 1983. The report describes in abundant detail the landing and departure of an unearthly spacecraft.

When journalists tried to interview Lt. Col. Halt, he took evasive action, but they finally caught up with him. At first he refused to discuss the matter, on the grounds that it could jeopardize his career, but then tacitly admitted that he had written and signed the report.

According to Andrews, journalists questioned Halt's commanding officer after the report appeared in print. The officer, Brigadier General Gordon Williams, said that he did not believe that Halt was the kind of person "who would hoax the British Ministry of Defence or the American Air Force Department."

Perhaps you have heard or read about other stories of people being contacted by aliens, or even of people being kidnapped and taken aboard spaceships. If so, you have probably wondered and asked yourself, "Are the stories true?" You also might have asked, "What are UFOs? Where do they come from? Do extraterrestrials, alien beings from space, really exist?"

Maybe you have seen an object in the sky at some time that you could not identify. Maybe it was bright

In a scene from the movie *E.T.*, Elliot says goodbye to his alien friend. Could an alien like E.T. exist?

or colored or was shaped like a football or cigar. It may have moved at an incredible speed and in all directions, up and down, forward and backward. It may have frightened you. If you could not identify something whirling around in the sky, you might speculate that it came from outer space. This is exactly what numerous people have thought.

Dubbed the California Great Airship, this version of the ship was supposed to have passed over Sacramento, Oakland, and San Francisco in November of 1896. It was reported to be oblong in shape and to have propellers and powerful searchlights.

Centuries-Old Belief

In fact, sightings of UFOs and a belief that other civilizations exist in space have been reported for centuries. In the eighteenth century, Bernard de Fontenelle argued that beings lived on Mercury and Mars. Author Jacques Vallee quotes de Fontenelle in *UFOs in Space*: Mercurians "must be fools because of their excessive vivacity." On Saturn "the inhabitants are so dull that it takes them a whole day to comprehend and answer a question." Obviously de Fontenelle had a fertile imagination! He based his ideas not on evidence but on what people thought was true about the planets.

Thomas Burnet, an English clergyman, wrote in the seventeenth century: "If instead of crossing the Seas we could waft [sail] ourselves over to our neighboring Planets, we should meet with such varieties there, both in Nature and in Mankind, as would very enlarge our thoughts and Souls."

At the same time, many people throughout history have argued against the idea that other inhabited worlds exist. Alfred Russel Wallace, the English naturalist, wrote in the nineteenth century, "The old idea that all the planets were inhabited, and that all the stars existed for the sake of other planets, which planets existed to develop life, would, in the light of our present knowledge, seem utterly improbable and incredible." In other words, to think that life exists on other planets is foolish! William Whewell, English philosopher, mathematician, and professor at Cambridge University in England, was also skeptical. He wrote, also in the nineteenth century, that the people

This illustration comes from a broadsheet by Swiss scholar Samuel Coccius, an eyewitness and skeptic, who wrote, "On the 7th of August before and at sunrise, numerous large black spheres were seen in the sky. Suddenly they started racing toward the sun with great speed. . . . Several were also seen to turn fiery red and then they vanished."

who believed other inhabited worlds exist were assuming too much without supportive evidence.

There was a time in history when believing in the existence of other worlds could cause a person to be imprisoned or put to death. Giordano Bruno, for example, was burned at the stake in Rome on February 17, 1600. He dared to think that there was life elsewhere and that the Earth was not the center of the universe. He was put to death by the Roman Catholic church after serving six years in prison. Why? One of the church's beliefs at that time was that the universe was finite, which means limited in size. According to the church, only God could be infinite, or unlimited. Therefore, nothing in the material world could be infinite, for this would challenge God's special place. This was one of the reasons that Bruno lost his life.

Early Beliefs in Extraterrestrial Life

Thomas R. McDonough, in his book *The Search for Extraterrestrial Intelligence,* quotes Bruno: "I hold the universe to be infinite, as being the effect of infinite divine power and goodness, of which any finite world would have been unworthy. Hence I have declared infinite worlds to exist beside this our Earth." Interestingly enough, Bruno was not challenging God's position in the scheme of things. He was merely challenging what the church wanted him to believe. Bruno thought there were other suns, planets, and beings in the universe: "Innumerable suns exist. Innumerable earths revolve about the suns in a manner similar to the way planets revolve around the sun. Living beings inhabit these worlds."

The notion that we are not alone in the universe goes back to the early Greeks. Edward Edelson, in *Who Goes There?,* says that Anaximander, a Greek astronomer in the sixth century B.C., thought there could be other planets. And Metrodorus, a Greek philosopher in the fourth century B.C., said: "To consider Earth as the only populated world is as absurd as to assert that in an entire field sown with millet only one grain will grow.'' Edelson thinks that this fourth century B.C. statement could summarize today's view about life in the universe.

''We may learn, soon perhaps, that we are only one tiny part of a Grand Family of humans stretching to the remotest star.''

Spacegod theorists and authors Max H. Flindt and Otto O. Binder, *Mankind—Child of the Stars*

UFOs in the Bible?

Any investigation of UFOs will show that there are many ideas about the phenomenon. It has even been suggested that UFOs were referred to in the Bible. The following passage appeared in the *Australian Flying Saucer Review:*

> According to Genesis 19:3 Lot took the two angels he met at the gate of Sodom to his house ''and made them a feast, and did bake unleavened bread, and they did eat.'' But according to dictionary definitions, angels are spiritual, ethereal beings. Angels who ate with Lot could not have been such beings.
>
> Rev. H. Wipprecht of Cobalt, Canada, says that the Bible's description of angels fits ''intelligent beings'' from other planets. In the Old Testament these ''mysterious messengers'' were said to regularly visit the Earth from the sky, and on occasion actually intermarried with human beings. The angels who married earth women could not have been ''heavenly spirits.''

''The idea that thousands of advanced civilizations are scattered throughout the Galaxy is quite implausible.''

Author Michael H. Hart, from the paper *Extraterrestrials: Where Are They?*

Was the Bible talking about space beings, or angels? What is your interpretation?

What do we know about UFOs and extraterrestrials today? Some people think that other civilizations do exist in the universe. Others say there is still no evidence that they do. Before we consider the possibility of extraterrestrial life and whether there is evidence to support this belief, let us review some of what we know about how life begins.

One

Is There Life in Space?

Opposite page:
Six panels illustrating the six days of creation from a fifteenth-century Florentine woodcut.

There are two major theories about the origin of life. One theory is called the *creationist* view. It is based on a literal reading of the Christian Bible. Simply put, creationists believe that God took six days to create the earth. On the first day, God created light. Between the first and sixth day, the land, sea, plants, trees, animals, birds, and finally human beings were created. And on the seventh day God rested.

The other theory is known as the *evolutionary* view. It was proposed by the naturalist Charles Darwin who wrote *Origin of Species* in 1859. Darwin observed that life was evolutionary in nature. That is, one form of life evolved or changed into another form. Darwin stated in his book that all the animals and plants now on the planet have ancestors that go back to the beginning of time.

Most scientists today believe that evolution, or a combination of creation and evolution, best explains how life originated. However, some people still believe that the religious view is the true one.

Thomas R. McDonough, in his book *The Search for Extraterrestrial Intelligence,* provides an amusing description of the origin of life: "If there was a *Cosmic Cookbook of Life*, written by some galactic Julia Child, it would probably read something like this: Take one medium-size planet, place it near an average star. Add water, ammonia, methane, perhaps a dash of carbon dioxide. Turn on the electricity in the form of light-

DI UNO
DI SE GUNDO
DI TERZO
DI QUARTO
DI QUINTO
DI SESTO

"I believe that Man's progress on planet Earth has been monitored by beings whose technological and mental resources make ours look primitive."

Author Timothy Good, *Above Top Secret: The Worldwide UFO Coverup*

"The idea that Earth is under more or less constant, or even sporadic, surveillance by interstellar spacecraft . . . is simply preposterous."

Astrophysicist Donald H. Menzel and psychoanalyst Ernest H. Taves, *The UFO Enigma*

ning. Stir. Wait patiently—a few hundred million years will do. Then something will start swimming around in your soup—you may enjoy eating it. Or vice versa."

McDonough believes that knowing how life began here on earth will help us estimate the chances of life occurring on other planets that may exist outside our solar system.

Well-known scientist Carl Sagan talks about the origin of life in his book *Cosmos.* He explains that the process of life evolving into the forms we know today—including ourselves—took billions of years. Indeed, Sagan admits: "We are the products of a long series of biological accidents."

Could the same process have taken place on other planets? According to Ian Ridpath in his book *Messages from the Stars,* "Some scientists believe the emergence of life is very likely on suitable planets, while others think it would be rare." Sagan is optimistic that accidents could occur elsewhere. "There's no reason to think that we are the first or the last or the best," he says.

Intelligence in Space

If there is life in space, is it intelligent? Sagan speculates on this question: "Perhaps many stars have planetary systems rather like our own: at the periphery, great gaseous ringed planets and icy moons, and nearer to the center, small, warm, blue-white, cloud-covered worlds. On some, intelligent life may have evolved, reworking the planetary surface in some massive engineering enterprise. These are our brothers and sisters in the Cosmos. Are they very different from us?"

If reports about extraterrestrial visitations to earth are true, aliens at least *look* different. UFO researcher Richard Sigismond, in an interview that appeared in the *Daily Camera,* Boulder, Colorado, on November 3, 1985, summarized the descriptions various witnesses have given of aliens:

> There is a one meter [39.37 inches] tall entity, hairless, [with] large heads. A five-foot group with features one might call Eurasian is reported only occasionally. Nor is the creature with the long, spindly body—like the one in Spielberg's movie [*Close Encounters of the Third Kind*]—reported very often. One group of three-footers has thick bodies and pumpkin-shaped heads. . . . Then there are the 4½ foot humanoids [beings resembling humans]. They have grey skin tone, elongated heads, slight protuberances in place of ears, long claw-like hands.

Whitley Strieber, in his book *Communion: A True Story,* claims to have been abducted by aliens on December 26, 1985, from his cabin in upstate New York. He describes not only what the aliens looked like, but also how they acted.

> I was aware that I had seen four different types of figures. The first was the small robotlike being that led the way into my bedroom. He was followed by a large group of short, stocky ones in the dark-blue coveralls. These had wide faces, appearing either dark gray or dark blue in that light, with glittering deep-set eyes, pug noses, and broad, somewhat human mouths. Inside the room, I encountered two types of creatures that did not look at all human. The most

Scientist Carl Sagan (center) with Steven Spielberg (right). Spielberg is director of *E.T.* and *Close Encounters of the Third Kind*. Sagan, Spielberg and others are shown at Harvard University in 1985 at the turning on of the META system. The system uses a radio telescope to search for signs of intelligent life in the universe.

provocative of these was about five feet tall, very slender and delicate, with extremely prominent and mesmerizing black slanted eyes. This being had an almost vestigial mouth and nose. The huddled figures in the theater [operating room, where the figures took him] were somewhat smaller, with similarly shaped heads but round, black eyes like large buttons.

Later in his book, Strieber describes the aliens' movements as "stiff and insectlike" and says that they looked like "bugs."

In addition, Strieber speculates on their behavior:

> If the visitors are indeed insectlike they could be organized as a hive. . . . It could be that there is very little sense of self associated with individual members of their species. Taken together they might be very formidable, but separate individuals may be almost negligible. . . . One of the greatest biological mysteries is how hives function, and whether or not a hive can have a group mind.

An artist's depiction of the aliens Whitley Strieber says abducted him.

What Strieber seems to be suggesting is that the aliens did not have individual intelligence but a group intelligence that guided their actions.

Although Carl Sagan does not claim to have seen an extraterrestrial, he thinks that it is likely that the evolutionary process "should create extraterrestrial creatures very different from any we know." In short, Sagan thinks other life may exist. However, there is no guarantee it will be like us or even intelligent.

Other scientists seem certain that intelligent life does not exist outside the earth. One, biologist George Gaylord, wrote in a 1964 issue of *Science* magazine that the chances of life evolving into intelligent beings as it did on earth is zero. He doubted that the events that led to intelligence could ever happen accidentally again even here.

It could be though, that we are not the only life. The chemicals that make up life—hydrogen, helium, carbon, sulfur, among others—are said to be found all over the universe. It seems logical that these basic ingredients, given enough time, would produce life again.

Enrico Fermi, the Italian atomic physicist, gives a lecture in 1949.

"Certainly there are other civilizations, perhaps thousands of times older and wiser. And I believe intelligent beings from these civilizations are visiting us in spacecraft."

Aeronautical historian Charles Harvard Gibbs-Smith, *Flying Saucer Menace*

"It should be possible for a single civilization to colonize the entire galaxy in roughly ten million years. . . . Why has not one of them progressed to this stage? The logical conclusion would seem to be that it is because we are alone in the galaxy."

Author and UFO skeptic Robert Sheaffer, *The UFO Verdict: Examining the Evidence*

If life elsewhere in the universe has evolved into intelligent beings with an advanced technology, scientist Enrico Fermi asked, then where are they? Author Thomas McDonough sums up some of the possibilities:

> One possibility is that they *have* been here, but didn't see any interesting tourist attractions a billion years ago, and so left.
>
> Another possibility is that they seeded life. . . .We are then their descendants.
>
> Yet another possibility was once suggested jokingly by [British physicist] Thomas Gold: Maybe they landed before life arose, dumped their trash, took off, and the contamination from the trash was the seed of life which later evolved into us. This is sometimes known as the Garbage Hypothesis.

Scientists Carl Sagan and William Newman suggest that the galaxy is too big and maybe the space people are not here—yet. Or perhaps, says McDonough, "they are here *right now,* but don't want to make themselves known."

Civilizations in Space

Scientists estimate that there could be millions of other civilizations besides ours. There could be 10^{22} planets. That is 10,000,000,000,000,000,000,000 planets! How could there be so many? Look at it this way: Our earth is one of at least nine planets circling our sun. This is called a *solar system*. Our solar system is in a galaxy, the Milky Way. In our galaxy alone, there are billions and billions of stars. They are really just suns like ours but of different sizes and ages. Some of these suns may have planets like ours. Beyond our galaxy, there are billions of other galaxies, each with billions of stars, some of which may have planets. In this vast, multi-starred universe, why couldn't there be other planets where life exists?

Moreover, some life-forms might not even need planets to live on! Astronomer Sir Fred Hoyle and writer N.C. Wickramasinghe have theorized that life's

molecules could be created in the gas and dust clouds that are found between stars. This means that clouds could contain life! Imagine how trying it would be, attempting to speak to a cloud!

Clouds or no clouds, scientists have found indirect evidence that other planets do exist. They are invisible at this time though. They are too far away to be seen even through our most powerful telescopes. Scientists have reasons to believe they exist. One is that a planet's gravity affects the motion of its sun. This motion can be detected and measured by astronomers who study objects in space. So when scientists detect certain kinds of movement by a sun, they can be reasonably certain that the sun has planets.

Not Everyone Agrees

Still, none of this proves that life truly exists elsewhere. Opinions are divided. Michael H. Hart, from the National Center for Atmospheric Research in Colorado, has said that he does not think other intelligent life exists. Why not? Because if other civilizations exist, they should be not only capable of interstellar flight (space travel) but also capable of

The great galaxy Andromeda, one of the nearest galaxies to us and quite similar to our own Milky Way.

Prolific science fiction writer Isaac Asimov.

colonizing space. Since we have not encountered any aliens, he says, then logically speaking they do not exist.

One response to Hart is that if other beings do exist in space, the distance between them and us might be too far to travel unless they have discovered a means to travel faster than the speed of light.

Astronomers use the speed of light to measure distance in space. Light travels at 186,000 miles per second. The distance light travels over one year is six trillion miles. According to Carl Sagan in *Cosmos,* "If there are millions of civilizations distributed more or less randomly through the Galaxy, the distance to the nearest is about two hundred light-years [or twelve hundred trillion miles]. Even at the speed of light it would take two centuries for a radio message to get from there to here."

Scientist and writer Isaac Asimov agrees. He wrote in *Extraterrestrial Civilizations* that it is probable that great numbers of extraterrestrial civilizations exist, "but we have *not* been visited by them, very likely because interstellar distances are too great to be penetrated."

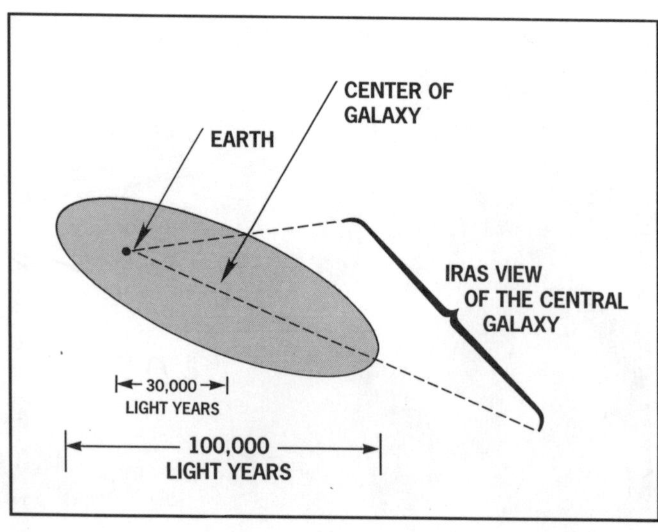

NASA graph showing the Earth in relation to the Milky Way. Earth is 30,000 light years from the center. The IRAS is the infrared space telescope.

Carl Sagan has come up with an interesting theory that, if true, could explain how UFOs could travel across the great distances of space. He talks about *black holes*. Black holes are stars that have collapsed into themselves. In other words, these stars have condensed. Neither light nor matter can escape from them. Sagan theorizes that they might actually be shortcuts through time and space. We might one day be able to travel into and out of them as if they were rapid transit systems through the universe. Do UFOs and extraterrestrials use black holes to travel throughout the universe? Maybe someday we shall find out.

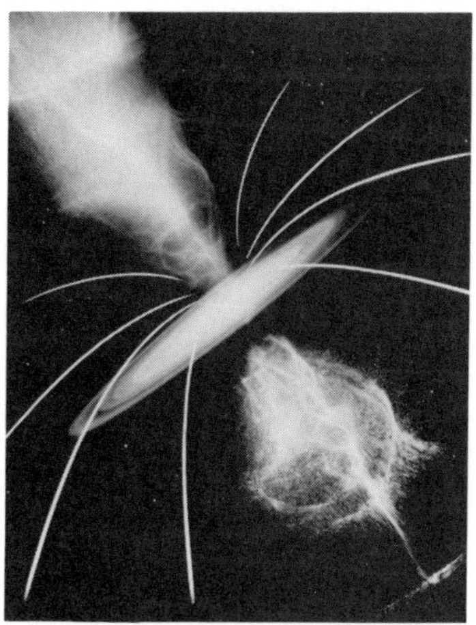

An invisible black hole at the center of a quasar is shown by a whirling disk of gas and dust that is being sucked into the hole, and by emissions of incredible energy (skeins of light). The curved lines demonstrate how space and time are distorted by the hole's gravitational pull.

The Search for Extraterrestrial Intelligence

Human technology is not yet advanced enough to travel to the stars and explore for other civilizations. However, scientists have tried to find ways we might at least be able to communicate with space beings. To date, radio communication seems the most promising means of sending or receiving signals to and from space.

The first person to propose that radio signals might be the way extraterrestrials would attempt to reach us was inventor and radio pioneer Nikola Tesla of Colorado. In 1900, he received signals on his primitive radio equipment, signals he believed came from space.

Nikola Tesla in his laboratory around 1910.

Karl G. Jansky of Bell Telephone Laboratories stands with the rotating antenna he used to discover radio waves coming from space. During the 1930s Jansky investigated strange noises in telephone equipment and discovered radiation noise from the center of the Milky Way. He gave us the new science of radio astronomy.

In *Messages from the Stars,* Ian Ridpath cites Tesla as saying, "The changes I noted were taking place periodically, and with such a clear suggestion of number and order that they were not traceable to any cause then known to me. . . . It was some time afterward that the thought flashed upon my mind that the disturbances I had observed might be due to intelligent control." Did Tesla actually receive intelligent signals from aliens? We have no way of knowing for sure. All we know is what he later reported—that he had received what seemed to be *patterned* radio signals from space.

The idea of radio communication with extraterrestrials really became popular around 1959. Two scientists, Giuseppe Cocconi and Philip Morrison, speculated that communication across space could best be accomplished by radio signals. (Scientists say that radio waves are more practical than building massive, complex spaceships, and they are less damaging to national pocketbooks!)

In 1967, a team of radio-astronomers headed by Dr. Anthony Hewish in England thought—briefly—that they had detected another civilization. They were

The VLA, Very Large Array, of the National Astronomical Observatory is a complex of twenty-seven mobile radio telescopes. Each radio telescope is twenty-five meters (eighty-two feet) in diameter. Engineers and scientists from VLA and NASA's Jet Propulsion Laboratory are preparing the VLA to support the Voyager 2 encounter with Neptune.

using radio telescopes, dish antennae similar to ones we use to pick up television signals. These are designed to pick up radio signals. Hewish's team began picking up regular series of signals unlike anything that had ever been received before from space.

Scientists and the public were excited. Were the signals some planet's hit tunes being broadcast over cosmic radio waves? A news bulletin? Or a Mayday message from a dying civilization? Some people thought the signals were being sent by "little green men"—the *LGM theory*, as it was called. According to McDonough, however, arguments were posed against the LGM theory. One objection was that no extraterrestrial civilization could generate the huge amounts of energy that the signals radiate. McDonough says that this energy would be more than the "entire electrical production of Earth."

Alas, investigation proved the signals not to be signs of life, but the natural signals of a previously unknown phenomenon, now called a *pulsar.* If you can visualize the way a lighthouse has a blinking light, then you can imagine what it means to pulsate.

Space "Heartbeats"

The pulsars that Hewish's team found came from a fixed point in the sky. This automatically ruled out the possibility that the signals were actually like satellites or man-made objects circling the earth. They also had a definite, unique sound. Thomas McDonough, in *The Search for Extraterrestrial Intelligence,* says: "Listening to pulsar signals is a strangely moving experience. The slowest pulsars sound just like the beating of a human heart, and you can't help at first wondering if these are the sounds of an inconceivably advanced alien civilization, received on Earth centuries after their broadcast."

Scientist Thomas Gold theorized (and it was later proven) that pulsars are spinning neutron stars. A neutron star is an incredibly compressed form of matter. What is compressed matter? Have you ever pressed down the trash in your garbage can with your foot? Then you know what compressed matter is. A neutron star is the same kind of thing, only on a vastly larger scale.

Gold's theory became the accepted one for pulsars. They are not messages from aliens. They are spinning stars that throw off signals because of their motion.

However, radio-astronomers still listen to the skies. In fact, in 1977, a new kind of signal was heard and recorded at Ohio State University on a radio telescope. It's known as the *Wow* signal. It only occurred once, but very strongly, and its origin was unknown. Was it from an intelligent source in outer space? Or was it a natural phenomenon like a pulsar?

Are radio signals really the best way to communicate with aliens? According to Ian Ridpath

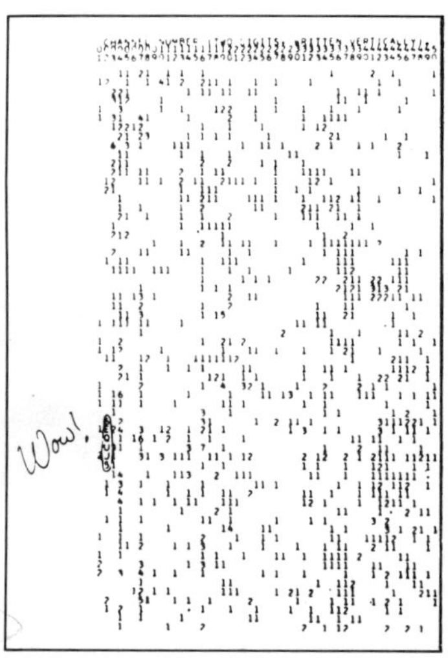

This is the "Wow" signal recorded at Ohio State University's radio observatory in 1977. The numbers represent the normal background noise of the sky, but the circled letters on the left indicate a very strong signal which could not be identified.

in *Messages from the Stars,* Gerrit Verschuur, a former radio-astronomer, was one of the first to look for signals coming from space. He believed he was wasting his time trying to communicate with aliens by radio. Ian Ridpath explained why. He said that if the basic scientific theories are true, the nearest possible civilization would be about two thousand light-years away.

> Even if we could find this nearest civilization among the tens of millions of stars within this radius, the travel time for a radio message each way would be two thousand years, and the round-trip time for an exchange of greetings would be four thousand years. But such a two-way conversation could never take place, because the lifetime of each civilization is too short—the line would go dead before the reply could be received.

Even if we received a message from space, would we be able to decipher it? Gerrit Verschuur is not too positive about that either. He points out that no two societies are likely to be at the same stage of development. Even if in thousands of years from now apes

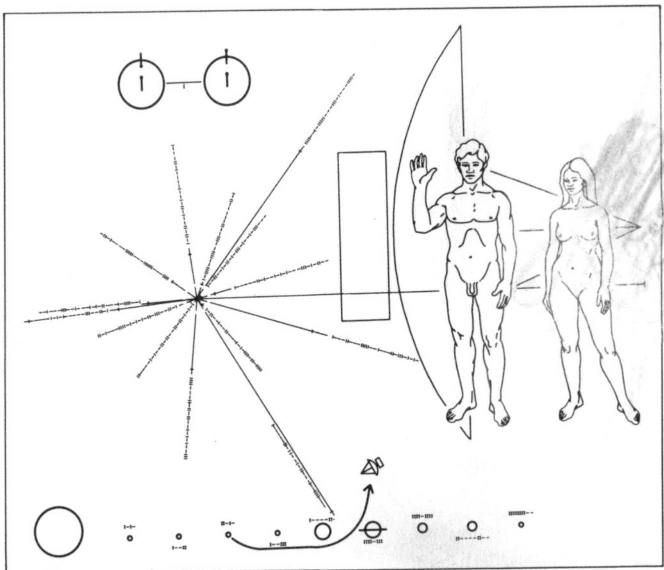

The Pioneer F spacecraft, launched in 1972, carries this pictorial plaque as a message for "scientifically educated inhabitants of some other star system" who might intercept it millions of years from now. The picture indicates our sun as the home star of our civilization with radiating lines indicating pulsars. The man and woman represent the creatures that created Pioneer. The man's hand is raised in goodwill. Across the bottom are all the planets in our system.

have evolved the ability to talk, we would probably not be able to understand them, for our own language would have evolved and changed. By the time ape language gets to where ours is now, ours would have changed considerably.

Maybe the language barrier will not be so great as in Verschuur's example, though. Ian Ridpath says that "we already can communicate in simple form with chimpanzees: The famous chimp Washoe was taught sign language used by the deaf and [mute], and another chimp, Sarah, was taught a language using colored plastic shapes for words."

Communications in Space

Will we ever be able to communicate with civilizations in space? We don't know, but one thing is certain. The messages that scientists have sent out will not be received by extraterrestrials for a long time.

In 1974, Cornell University scientists transmitted a message to space from the radio-telescopes at Arecibo, Puerto Rico. The message contained a description of humans, and also information regarding our biological chemistry. It was beamed to the constellation Hercules, named after the mythological Greek, which is twenty-five thousand light-years away.

Here is an aerial view of the radio telescopes at Arecibo, Puerto Rico.

Since the message was sent as a radio signal and radio signals travel at the speed of light, if anyone ever receives it, it will be after twenty-five thousand earth years have passed. Nothing alive on earth at this time will be alive then. Will a response be of value to us? If it is ever received, we will not even know it.

Science and UFOs

To summarize the attitudes of science toward UFOs and extraterrestrial beings: First, scientists agree that due to the sheer number of stars and galaxies, life surely could exist in space. Second, most scientists, however, think that UFOs are bunk. There just has not been enough evidence to prove that UFOs come from outer space.

What would constitute good evidence? Perhaps an alien body or spacecraft. In fact, UFO skeptic Philip Klass has offered to pay ten thousand dollars to anyone who can provide conclusive evidence of a UFO. The evidence must be confirmed in the following ways:

1. The U.S. National Academy of Sciences expresses the opinion that a crashed spacecraft, or a major part of one, is clearly identifiable as being of extraterrestrial origin.

2. The same group announces its opinion that other evidence conclusively proves that earth has been visited in the twentieth century by extraterrestrial spacecraft.

3. The first extraterrestrial visitor, born on a celestial body other than earth, appears live before the General Assembly of the United Nations or on national television.

So far, Klass has kept his ten thousand dollars. But, as has already been suggested, perhaps the extraterrestrials are hiding. Or, perhaps they do not want their presence revealed to everyone on television.

''One may argue that space flight is not the most cost-effective way to communicate between civilizations and that interstellar radio contact is a better way.''

Astronomer Carl Sagan, *UFOs: A Scientific Debate*

''A background of radio noise—'swishes,' 'whistles,' 'tweeks,'— come in constantly from the universe at large. Deliberate signals, if they occurred, would be hard to distinguish from the random noise.''

Astrophysicist Donald H. Menzel, *The World of Flying Saucers*

Two

Did Extraterrestrials Visit Earth in Ancient Times?

Opposite is a South American ceramic figure representing the type of alien that Erich von Däniken and Maurice Chatelain believe came to Earth and perhaps helped populate it.

Some writers have suggested that at the beginning of civilization earth was visited by aliens. They even think it is possible that our ancestors were aliens who mated with early humans. According to writer Erich von Däniken, because our ancestors had contact with extraterrestrials, humanity advanced from savages to civilized peoples. Some other von Däniken theories are these:

• we are the descendants of space colonists;

• we are the result of crossbreeding between space people and the higher apes;

• we are a result of genetic experiments by aliens (This is an interesting idea, for science is aware that there is a "missing link" between two species of our ancestors—Neanderthal man and Cro-Magnon man.);

• aliens used the earth as a penal colony or perhaps a mental institution—this would mean that we are the descendants of criminals and lunatics!

Another writer, Maurice Chatelain in his book *Our Ancestors Came from Outer Space,* says:

> Once upon a time, about sixty-five thousand years ago, extraordinary visitors came from another civilization in space, discovered the earth was a wonderful place to live on, and decided to establish a colony here. But in the beginning they did not like

An old woodcut gives us an idea of what Neanderthal man may have looked like.

our air and water, and they weren't used to earth's gravity. So, these visitors decided to create a hybrid race, so that crossbreeding with humans after a few generations, that new race would be perfectly adapted to life on earth and would carry on at least part of the intelligence and technical know-how of its ancestors from space. To achieve this, the most attractive and the most intelligent young females were inseminated [fertilized], and this procedure continued with their daughters and granddaughters until the results were acceptable for life on earth, and the education and civilization of the new race could start.

What did these ancient visitors look like, assuming they in fact visited earth? We cannot be certain, but if we speculate that they mated with the Neanderthal species and produced the Cro-Magnon species, which evolved into modern humans, they may have looked similar to Neanderthals. At least they would have had larger heads than we do. It is known that Neanderthal and Cro-Magnon humans had larger skulls than modern humans. Therefore, the aliens would probably have had larger brains, too.

Chatelain also says that knowledge was passed on to humanity by astronauts from outer space who created modern humans. "Our primitive ancestors were thus quickly transformed from Neanderthal men into Cro-Magnon men, the strong and intelligent beings that appeared on earth about sixty-five thousand

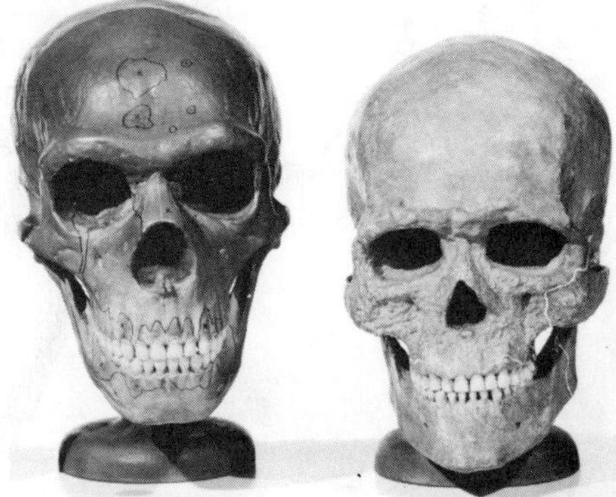

These two skulls of a Neanderthal (left) and a Cro-Magnon (right) show relative head size.

years ago.'' Chatelain believes that space beings were responsible for teaching earthlings to chart the skies, make calendars, and build pyramids. However, the scientific view is that ancient peoples had not even invented the wheel.

"The entire episode related in the book of Ezekiel can perfectly reasonably be attributed to the report of a contemporary-type ufonaut landing in the Sinai desert.''

Author Paris Flammonde, *UFOs Exist!*

Alien Ancestors

Could aliens have been our ancestors? Did they actually breed with earth women? According to Carl Sagan in his book *The Cosmic Connection*, these claims are sad stories. He thinks the stories are fantasies, especially those that state that sexual mating between extraterrestrials and humans occurred: "Such crossings are about as reasonable as the mating of a man and a petunia.''

"The two famous visions of the prophet Ezekiel were in fact singularly accurate descriptions . . . of a phenomenon well known to meteorologists, technically called 'parhelia.'''

Astrophysicist and former director of the Harvard College Observatory Donald H. Menzel in, *UFOs: A Scientific Debate*

Yet sometimes even the Bible is used as evidence that earth was visited by aliens. One of the prophets, Ezekiel, is said to have described aliens and UFOs in a vision. Von Däniken in his book *Chariots of the Gods?* relates the story:

> Now it came to pass in the thirtieth year, in the fourth month, in the fifth day of the week, as I was among the captives by the river of Chebar, that the heavens were opened. . . . And I looked, and, . . . a whirlwind came out of the north, a great cloud, and a fire [folding into] itself, and a brightness was about it, and out of the midst . . . as the color of amber, out of the midst of the fire. Also out of the midst . . . came the likeness of four living creatures. And this was their appearance: They had the likeness of a man. And every one had four faces, and every one had four wings. And their feet were straight feet; and the sole of their feet was like the sole of a calf's foot; and they sparkled like the color of burnished brass.

Von Däniken claims the above passage describes the landing of a space vehicle. The more usual interpretation is that angels came and gave Ezekiel instructions on how to restore order to his country. But von Däniken questions that interpretation. If he is

This is one version of Ezekiel's vision showing the four creatures with human faces and four wings. Each is accompanied by a wheel. Do the wheels indicate a space vehicle?

right, the angels could have been aliens from some star in space.

Ronald D. Story in his book *Guardians of the Universe?*, takes issue with von Däniken. He says that von Däniken uses the Bible as an authority, but falsely "creates the illusion that the Bible is really just a straightforward account of spaceships landing and spacemen trotting all over the place, to give his audience everything it wants—Biblical truth combined with exciting adventures akin to Buck Rogers or Flash Gordon, presented as historical fact."

In a scene from *Flash Gordon Conquers the Universe*, made in 1939, Flash battles a robot alien. It may have been exciting to watch, but not very realistic.

Von Däniken makes other claims as well. For one, he believes ancient astronauts once landed high in the Peruvian mountains on a landing strip specifically built for spaceships. About two hundred fifty miles southeast of Lima, Peru, the Nazca, an ancient people, lived on a flat plateau. To this day, the ground is covered with thirteen thousand lines etched into the earth. There are at least one hundred geometrical shapes consisting of spirals, trapezoids, and triangles. They can be seen from the air. Also there are about eight hundred animal figures etched into the ground. The lines and animals are estimated to have been made between 400 B.C. and A.D. 900. The plateau is about thirty-seven miles long and one mile wide.

If Not Runways, What?

Von Däniken says that archaeologists believe that the lines are Inca roads. (The Incas were a people that came after the Nazcas.) It is astonishing that anyone could think such a thing, von Däniken says. "Of what use to the Incas were roads that ran parallel to each other? That intersected?''

Why did the Nazcas etch these lines into the ground? What were they used for? Von Däniken says:

> Seen from the air, the clear-cut impression that the 37-mile-long plain of Nazca made on *me* was that of an airfield.
>
> In that case, what purpose did the lines at Nazca serve? According to my way of thinking, they could have been laid out on their gigantic scale by working from a model and using a system of coordinates, or they could also have been built according to instructions from an aircraft. It is not yet possible to say with certainty whether the plain of Nazca was ever an airfield. . . . What is wrong with the idea that the lines were laid out to say to the ''gods'': ''Land here! Everything has been prepared as you ordered''?

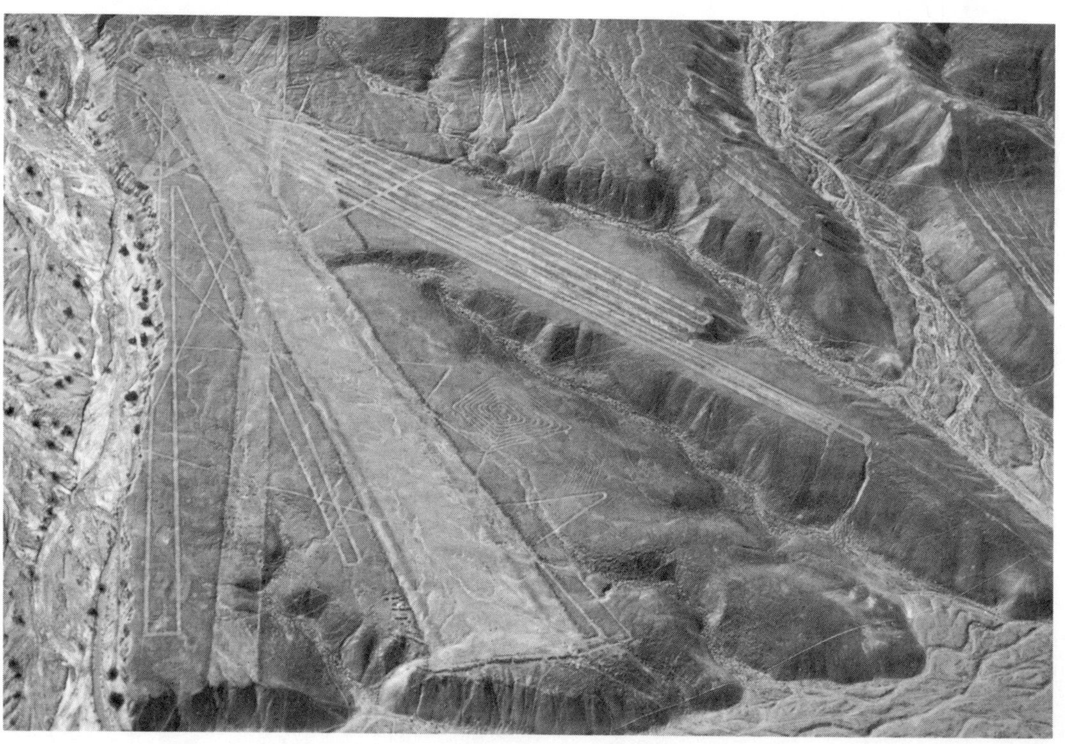

This photo gives us a unique view of a pre-Columbian Nazca civilization's system of lines and triangles on a mountain slope. The lines might be interpreted as a runway or as an astronomical calendar.

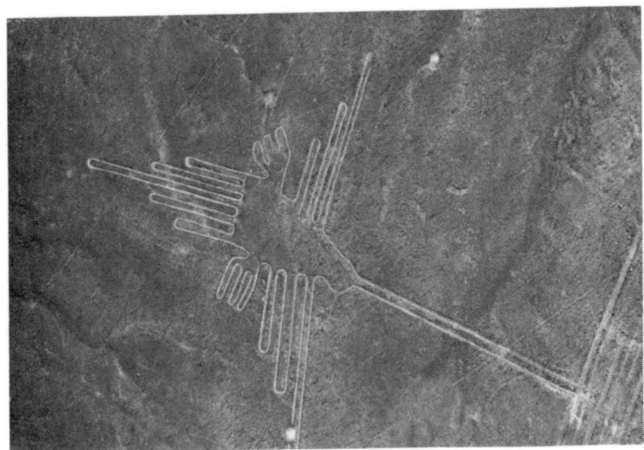

An aerial photo of one of the Nazca figures which resembles a hummingbird when seen from the air.

Ronald Story, however, has discovered some errors in von Däniken's thinking. He makes this point: If space vehicles could land vertically, why have a long horizontal runway? He also says that the soil on the plateau is too soft for a vehicle landing.

Story asks, "What, then, could have been the purpose of such an enormous array of lines, shapes, and animal figures created more than a thousand years ago?" To answer, he refers to evidence provided by professor Paul Kosok of Long Island University, who studied the site in 1941. Professor Kosok found one of the lines to be aligned with the setting sun of June 22, 1941. This is the day of the winter solstice in the southern hemisphere. The winter solstice is when the sun reaches its lowest point over the earth.

According to Story, Kosok also "confirmed more than a dozen such alignments, some for the solstices and others for the equinoxes. (An equinox is the time of year when the sun is at such a point in the sky that the length of day and of night are approximately equal.) This indicates that the Nazca 'landing field' very likely was a gigantic astronomical calendar and observatory."

But what about the difficulties the Nazcas had to experience to make markings only recognizable from

Jim Woodman and Julian Knott built a primitive balloon, called Condor I, to view the Nazca etchings. Although the balloon flew a distance of three miles in twenty minutes, the men had to abandon it shortly after takeoff. However, they did prove that it was possible for the Nazcans to have flown.

the air? Story says that the Nazcas might have had primitive hot air balloons.

Jim Woodman of the International Explorers Society wrote in his book, *Nazca: Journey to the Sun*, that graves containing braided rope and pottery were discovered in the area. On one piece of pottery, there was a picture that looked like a hot air bag with rope tied to it.

On November 28, 1975, Woodman and balloonist Julian Nott constructed a primitive hot air balloon out of the same materials that would have been available to the Nazcas. Then they flew in it over the plain. Helium was not available then. Did the Nazcas fly over just to see their artwork?

Donald H. Menzel and Ernest H. Taves in their book *The UFO Enigma* suggest that the lines might have been made for artistic, religious, or astronomical reasons. Perhaps the figures were meant to be seen from the sky. The people of certain ancient cultures believed that the gods were in the skies. Maybe the Nazcas built balloons just so they could supervise the drawing of the figures and lines. Perhaps they wanted to make the gods happy!

The Palenque Astronaut

Palenque, an ancient Mayan city, lies on the Yucatan Peninsula in Mexico. A seventy-foot limestone pyramid called the *Temple of Inscriptions* is located there. Ronald Story tells about this pyramid:

> Until 1949, the interior of the structure had remained unexplored. But when the Mexican archaeologist Alberto Ruz Lhullier noticed fingerholes in one of the large floor slabs, he raised the stone and discovered a hidden stairway that had been deliberately filled in, centuries ago, with stone and rubble and clay. After four years of clearing away the blockage, Ruz and his workers had descended sixty-five steps into the pyramid, where he came upon a secret tomb. Little did Ruz know that twenty years

Bas-relief on the tomb of Lord Pacal which von Däniken believes portrays an astronaut sitting at the controls of his space ship. Scientists state that the carvings represent the symbolic transition of a human soul to the realm of the dead. The figure reclines in front of and below a sacred tree which Mayans believed linked earth with the underworld and the heavens.

later his discovery would be used as one of the ''proofs'' of the existence of ancient astronauts.

What was this proof? On top of the tomb there is a stone carving, or bas-relief. Erich von Däniken and Maurice Chatelain have said that the stone carving is of an ancient astronaut. This is von Däniken's description:

> There sits a human being, with the upper part of his body bent forward like a racing motorcyclist; today any child would identify his vehicle as a rocket. . . . The crouching being himself is manipulating a number of indefinable controls and has the heel of his left foot on a kind of pedal. . . . The astronaut's front seat is separated by struts from the rear portion of the vehicle, in which symmetrically arranged boxes, circles, points, and spirals can be seen.

Von Däniken then asks: ''What does this [bas-] relief have to tell us? Nothing? Is everything that anyone links up with space travel a stupid figment of the imagination?''

Maurice Chatelain is as positive as von Däniken: ''The very well-preserved bas-relief depicted an astronaut sitting at the controls of a space vehicle! And it was unmistakably a spacecraft propelled by a jet

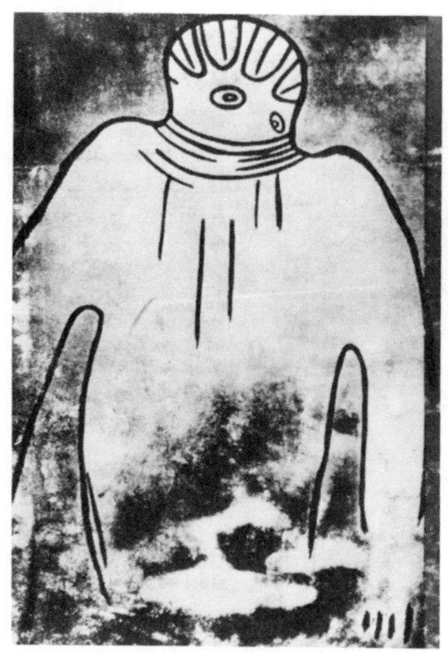

A figure in the Tassili frescoes which von Däniken used to support his argument for alien visitors to Earth. Archaeologists believe the figures are wearing ceremonial masks.

exhaust.'' Furthermore, Chatelain says, Ruz found a well-preserved white man in the tomb, who was about seventy inches tall. The average Mayan was sixty inches tall, or five feet. Did Ruz find the remains of an ancient astronaut? If they were taller than the average human of the time, in what other ways did they differ? Are von Däniken and Chatelain right?

Ronald Story, again, is not as certain that the carving depicts an astronaut. He believes the rocket is a composite artform: The sculpture seemed to be a cross between a two-headed serpent and corn leaves. ''The whole scene is a religious illustration, not a technological one, and is well understood within the proper context of Maya religious art.''

Cave Paintings

Then what about the Tassili cave paintings in northern Africa? These were discovered on the walls of a rocky gorge in the Tassili mountain range in the Sahara Desert. They are paintings of figures that von Däniken believes are spacemen, for they look like they are wearing divers' suits and antennae or helmets: ''Without overstretching my imagination, I get the impression that the great god Mars is depicted in a space or diving suit. On his heavy, powerful shoulders rests a helmet which is connected to his torso by a kind of joint . . . there are several of these clumsy figures with the same equipment at Tassili.''

Does Story agree with von Däniken about Tassili? ''What von Däniken calls a 'helmet' looks more like a sultan's turban, to me,'' Story says. ''Could it be possible that the clothing worn by the personage of that particular painting might in fact be a ritual mask or costume?''

The Crystal Skull

Another mysterious item that has been held up as evidence of ancient and extraterrestrial technology is the crystal skull. A reproduction of a human skull, it is almost life-size, and it is made of pure quartz crystal. It weighs eleven and a half pounds. According to legend, the skull has magical and psychic powers similar to those of a crystal ball.

Did aliens make the skull and leave it on earth long ago? If so, why? In his book, *The Ancient Visitors*, writer Daniel Cohen asks if the skull was "produced by an ancient but unknown technology? Indeed, is the skull really ancient at all?" According to Cohen, there is doubt. He says the skull first appeared in the possession of British adventurer F.A. Mitchell-Hedges in 1927. Although the adventurer never said exactly where he got the skull, Cohen says stories report that Mitchell-Hedges got the skull at a Mayan site in the Yucatan.

Moreover, according to Cohen, the crystal is not as ancient as believed. He says that archaeologists think the skull was made and cut in London in the late 1800s or early 1900s. Cohen says that the artifact is "one of the most exceptional carved gemstones in existence. But it is a work of art, not a marvel of technology either ancient or modern. A modern gem cutter of sufficient skill could produce such an object and a Mayan artisan could almost certainly have also."

Visitations to Other Planets

There is no clear agreement on whether or not extraterrestrials ever came to earth. But what about ancient astronauts having visited other planets? Did they visit Mars? What if, at one time, there were battles in the heavens?

UFO writer George C. Andrews, in his book *Extra-Terrestrials Among Us*, says that the legends of a "war in heaven" might be true. He explains that some of the craters on the moon and on Mars are in such definite patterns that they suggest nuclear warfare.

It could very well be that Andrew's idea is based on fact.

"I get the impression that the great god Mars is depicted in a space or diving suit. On his heavy powerful shoulders rests a helmet."

Author Erich von Däniken, *In Search of Ancient Gods*

"Why would space helmets be worn by persons who are otherwise naked? The vast majority of his 'space-suited' figures collected from all over the world are similarly 'depressurized.' These include the Tassili frescoes."

Author Ronald Story, *Guardians of the Universe?*

On Halloween, 1938, radio stations throughout the nation broadcast a radio play based on H.G. Wells's novel *War of the Worlds.* This science fiction story described Martians invading and taking over the planet earth. Millions of listeners believed the broadcast was true. Many panicked, sought shelter, or closed their homes. Of course, the story was a fictionalized one. Since NASA's *Viking* exploration probes landed on Mars on June 19 and August 7, 1976, we know that life does not exist there. At least, not *now.* But did life exist there in the past?

Science writer Richard C. Hoagland, in his book *The Monuments of Mars,* suggested that about five hundred thousand years ago, beings either lived on or visited Mars.

Why would anyone believe such an idea? When the *Viking* probes circled Mars, they took thousands of photographs. In some of those photographs, there appears to be a monument of some sort. It remarkably resembles a human face. It is located on a mesa that is one mile wide. There also appear to be pyramids on Mars.

Approximately two and one-half years after the *Viking* probes, someone suggested the face so ac-

With his arms upraised, Orson Welles directs the 1938 radio drama "War of the Worlds," which shocked and confused thousands of people.

Note the "face" in the huge Martian rock formation. NASA scientists say it is created by shadows which give the illusion of eyes, nose, and mouth.

curately depicts a human face that perhaps it was not just accidentally sculpted by Martian winds. But if the face is so remarkable, why didn't NASA officials notice it in the photographs in the first place? Richard Grossinger, publisher of *The Monuments of Mars,* describes how NASA reacted to the face:

> From its sudden unexpected appearance on a NASA data-tape [computer memory system], the Face has been the victim of one debunking after another. NASA didn't even give it the respect of looking twice; in the official collective mind, it had to be a mirage [an optical illusion]. The space agency squandered its major opportunity to go back and re-photograph the site while the one-board cameras were still functioning.

But Richard C. Hoagland speculated otherwise. Discounting the idea that the face was made by nature, Hoagland arrived at three other possible explanations: First, it was made by Martians, whoever or whatever they were. Second, it was made by visitors from outer space who constructed and left the face as a "calling card." Or third, a previous technological civilization on Earth went to Mars and perhaps beyond. They left the face as a message to the future.

Hoagland believes his third idea could be the closest to the truth. He maintains that "contrary to popular opinion, we know almost *nothing* about the

This 1905 map of Mars was drawn by Percival Lowell to show the canals he observed. He was convinced that intelligent life existed on Mars, but modern scientists say that the marks are optical illusions of Martian geographical features.

past history of our planet. . . . If all the plant and animal fossils ever found were stacked within one room, they would probably not fill an auditorium (the human remains would not cover a billiard table).''

Hoagland is suggesting that we cannot be certain about what occurred in the earth's history. Perhaps there *were* advanced civilizations on our planet at one time that for one reason or another migrated elsewhere by way of space travel. Indeed, there is a popular legend concerning an ancient land called Atlantis. Atlantis—if it ever existed—disappeared from the face of the earth thousands of years ago. One theory is that the Atlanteans may have destroyed themselves through atomic warfare. Perhaps some of them escaped into space.

Yet Hoagland admits that there is little concrete evidence to back up his third theory:

> From all the available evidence gathered by Mariner and Viking probes about the physical make-up of the planet, including its geological and

climatological history stretching back countless aeons to the past, the "Martians" who had created this amazing complex [structures on Mars] had to have disappeared ages before the human race—or even its ancestors—evolved.

How could a race of extinct beings create a monument to someone who would not appear in the same solar system—let alone the same planet—for several million years?

The mystery of the face lingers on. Richard Grossinger says the face is "a concrete object apparently carved from a Martian mesa in precise alignment to the sun and to surrounding structures." He adds that NASA did not recognize the artifacts "because they were not supposed to be there, [and] because they would have been too outrageous to believe." Yet Hoagland has found certain alignments between the face, the pyramids, and what he calls the *City,* a group of what appears to be deliberately built

"Disappointingly, Mars turned out to be as dead as a doornail—or more so. Even a doornail might be expected to have some organic matter on it, but the Martian soil has no complex organic molecules."

Astronomer William K. Hartman, *The Grand Tour: A Traveller's Guide to the Solar System*

"I haven't seen anything that makes me go negative on the idea of microbes on Mars."

Viking probe scientist Tobias Owen, *The Search for Life on Mars*

This is a model of the Viking Mars lander which collected samples from Mars. It is on display at the Jet Propulsion Laboratory.

structures. The precise alignments indicate to Hoagland that the Mars structures are more than nature's handiwork. In fact, Hoagland even asks if the face is an example of an extraterrestrial work of art. If so, why did the alien artisans make it look like a human face?

The Scientists

What does the scientific community think of the face on Mars? According to scientist George W. Enley in a review quoted in *The Monuments of Mars,* "the scientific community is skeptical." They believed that the object was made by the forces of nature.

In this shot from the 1953 movie *War of the Worlds*, we see the citizens approaching a crashed Martian space ship. At the right, a Martian extends its arm from an open porthole. Creators of science fiction want us to believe we are not alone in the universe.

In the near future, the mystery may be solved one way or another. Continuing space probes by the Soviets and the Americans will perhaps explore the face more thoroughly. If the evidence suggests that the face *was* made by extraterrestrials, what would it mean? Grossinger thinks the face "tells us we may not be alone and our destiny may be tied to the destiny of Others."

Who were, or are, the Others? Some people think that some of the Others never left earth, and that they are the occupants of the occasional UFOs reported around the world. In the following chapter we shall look at some UFO sightings.

Three

How Are UFOs Explained?

Kenneth Arnold (opposite) reported seeing nine circular objects while flying his plane. Arnold is credited with coining the term "flying saucers."

On Tuesday, June 24, 1947, experienced pilot Kenneth Arnold was flying a small plane in the state of Washington, near the Cascade Mountains. According to Arnold, as he was approaching Mt. Rainier he witnessed nine circular objects moving at high speed about twenty to twenty-five miles away. The objects flew in formation and swerved in and out among the mountain peaks.

Arnold landed in Oregon and told a reporter of his sighting. He said that the objects "flew like a saucer would if you skipped it across the water." He also was interviewed by the air force and said, "I could see their outline quite plainly as they approached the mountain. They flew very close to the mountaintops, flying like geese in a diagonal, chainlike line, as if they were linked together. They were flat like a pie-pan and so shiny that they reflected the sun like a mirror."

The story was reported across the nation, and the term "flying saucer" was born. Today we mostly call these mysterious objects UFOs—unidentified flying objects.

The truth is, UFOs were not a new phenomenon, but because of Arnold and the news story, they caught the attention of the whole country. What was it that

Arnold holds a drawing he made of the objects he saw. Light came from the dark spot at the center of the UFO.

Arnold saw? According to the air force, Arnold was either hallucinating—seeing things in his mind that weren't real—or else he was seeing a mirage, a distorted reflection of a distant object that results from atmospheric conditions.

Daniel Cohen has another possible explanation for Arnold's sighting. Cohen says he "may have seen clouds created by wind currents from the mountains, or an optical illusion resulting from unusual meteorological [weather] conditions."

Killed Chasing a UFO

Not long after Arnold saw his UFOs, an F-51 fighter pilot, Thomas Mantell, crashed and died chasing a UFO. On January 7, 1948, the air force base at Goodman in Kentucky got a call from state police that a UFO had been seen. Minutes later, the Air Force tower apparently saw a disklike object fly over the base. Three fighter planes scrambled in pursuit of the objects. One was flown by Mantell.

As Mantell climbed after the UFO, he radioed something like "I've sighted the thing. It looks metallic and tremendous in size. I'm at 10,000 feet and pursuing it." But minutes later, Mantell crashed. Why? Was he shot down by a UFO? The air force's

Lenticular clouds over Mt. Shasta in northern California, such as those often mistaken for flying objects.

immediate explanation was that Mantell had only seen the planet Venus, a bright object in the sky. They said that because of a lack of oxygen at the altitude he was flying, he blacked out and never regained consciousness.

Another theory about Mantell's object, offered by Donald H. Menzel in *Flying Saucers,* is that Mantell may have mistaken a mock sun for the object. A mock sun is an image that occurs in the sky caused by ice crystals floating in the atmosphere.

Daniel Cohen offers still another explanation. He says that what people probably saw that day was a giant balloon. The navy was then testing balloons for high-altitude reconnaissance.

Often UFO sightings are explained away like this. Daniel Cohen in his book *A Close Look at Close Encounters* writes, "It is perfectly possible for an honest person to see the planet Venus shining with extraordinary brightness and believe that he or she has seen a spaceship." But those who believe that UFOs are visitors from space bring up a good point

Old etching of a natural phenomenon showing two mock suns around the real sun.

An artist's depiction of Mantell and the other two pilots chasing a strange metallic object.

about the Mantell sighting and others like it: Why would a trained, experienced, *reliable* pilot have such an hallucination? (In the case of Thomas Mantell, it was later determined that Venus was actually so faint in the sky that day that it was hardly visible.)

Planetary objects are a common explanation for UFOs: What people see are really planets like Venus or Jupiter. In many cases, though, like Mantell's, the theory doesn't hold water.

UFOs in History

According to Jacques Vallee, astrophysicist and former NASA consultant, reports of UFOs date back to at least the second century B.C. Around that time a dozen sightings of strange objects in the skies were recorded. Prior to the twentieth century, there are written records of at least three hundred sightings from around the globe. Reports came from Chile, England, Italy, Mexico, France, Turkey, Vietnam, Australia, and other countries as well.

Throughout the centuries, many similarities show up in the descriptions of the sightings. More than a thousand years ago, according to Vallee, in 919 in Hungary, "spherical objects, shining like stars, bright and polished, were reported going to and fro in the

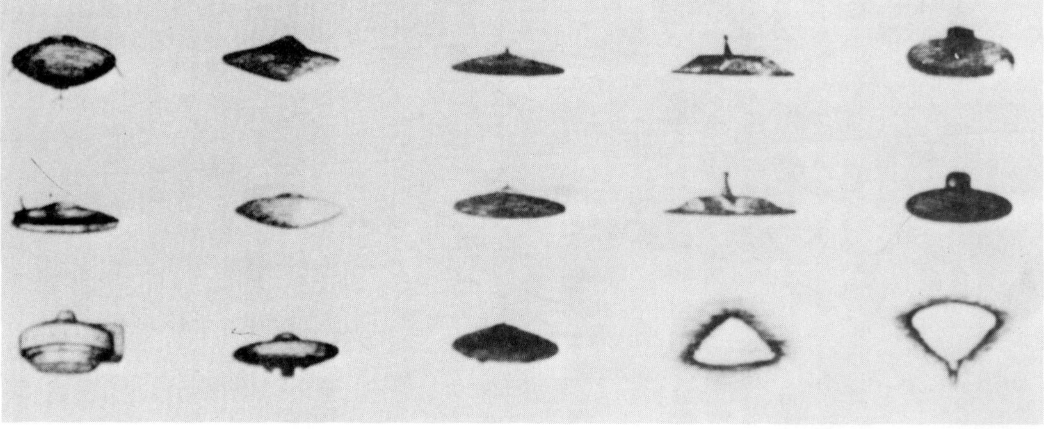

This is a portion of an illustration of commonly described UFO shapes which was entered into the Congressional Record.

sky.'' The numerous reports of UFOs in the nineteenth century described them as ''luminous bodies,'' ''fiery spheres,'' ''disks,'' ''wheels,'' ''circular,'' and ''celestial object.''

Descriptions of present-day UFOs often contain terms similar to those in the older reports. They are reported as ''disk-shaped,'' ''cigar-shaped,'' ''torpedo-shaped,'' ''cone-shaped,'' and ''ball-shaped.'' They are also reported to ''hover,'' to ''swing back and forth,'' to ''fly at high speeds,'' to ''rise vertically,'' to ''revolve on their axes,'' and to ''change shapes as they get closer.''

UFO writers have noted that sightings of the objects seem to happen in waves. That is, many sightings from varous places around the world are reported about the same time. A series of waves occurred between the 1880s and the early 1900s in Europe, Latin America, Great Britain, the Middle East, and the U.S. The next major waves weren't reported until the 1940s and 1950s in Scandinavia, Europe, Russia, and the U.S. Most recently, waves of UFO sightings have occurred in the American middle west.

Ufologists, those who study UFOs, aren't certain what causes these waves of sightings, but one suggestion is that they occur at dangerous times in the world's history. For example, one of the major waves occurred in the 1950s, not too long after the U.S.

Drawing made of an airship seen by Walter McCann north of Chicago on April 11, 1892.

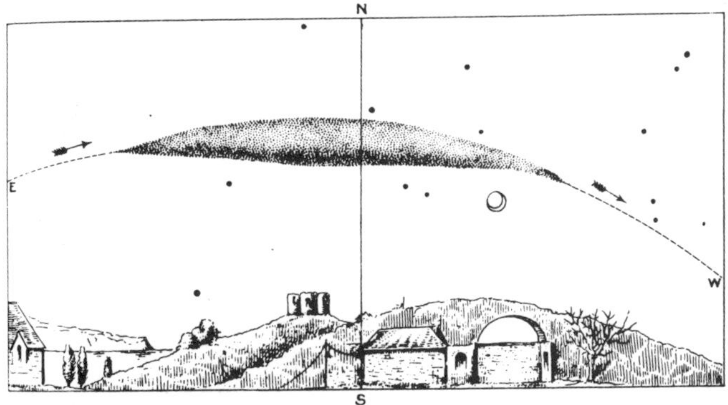

The Great Saucer of 1882 was seen in several places around the world in November 1882. There was a well-documented very bright aurora at about the same time.

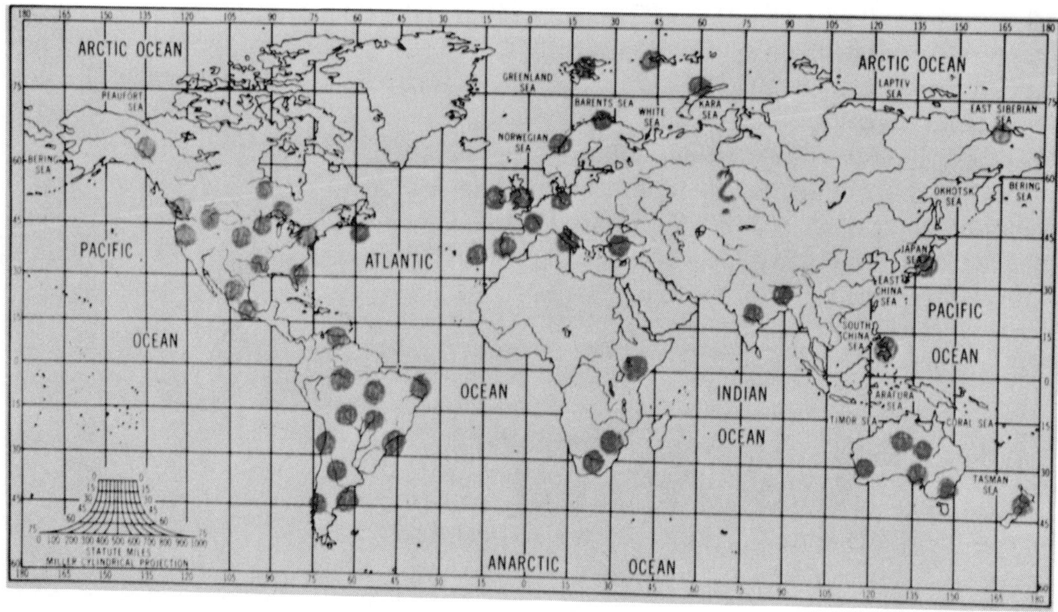

World map of UFO sightings.

dropped atomic bombs on Nagasaki and Hiroshima, Japan, to end World War II. Writer Jacques Vallee, in *UFOs in Space: Anatomy of a Phenomenon*, reports that Dr. J. E. Lipp, scientist, was one of the first people to investigate the possibility that aliens were trying to contact humans, or at least observe us. Apparently he suggested that A-bombs might have alarmed the extraterrestrials and started a wave of sightings at that time.

Are space aliens concerned about the future of earth, or will a calamity here somehow affect their own existence? Or, are they like so many of us, attracted by tragedy—just like those people who slow down to view an accident on the highway?

Three Types of Sightings

UFO sightings have been classified according to three basic patterns:

• Close Encounter of the First Kind (CE I). The UFO is seen at close range but does not interact with the environment. This can happen either night or day.

Flattened reeds at a reported UFO landing site in Japan on August 8, 1986.

• Close Encounter of the Second Kind (CE II). The UFO does interact with the environment and causes a physical effect on plants, trees, animals, and humans. Vegetation is reported as being pressed down or scorched. Animals are frightened. Humans can suffer minor burns or cloudy thinking. Engines can stall, headlights dim, and home appliances stop.

• Close Encounter of the Third Kind (CE III). Alien beings are reported to be in or near a UFO. Abductions of humans occur.

There are many theories about UFOs. Let's take a look at some sightings (CE Is) and the explanations that have been offered for them.

Explanations

A popular one is that they come from outer space and are occupied by aliens. This is called the Extraterrestrial Hypothesis. Margaret Sachs, in her book *The UFO Encyclopedia,* says that the popularity of the theory may be due "to the twentieth century's space age interpretations of poorly understood phenomena and the human need to believe in a higher power."

Sachs says the weakest aspect of the theory revolves around the problem of interstellar travel. The

Mr. Spock holds a model of the Starship Enterprise in which the television characters of "Star Trek" made interstellar travel seem effortless and commonplace.

"The complement at Washington Airport radar facilities had said that what they had monitored 'were caused by radar waves' bouncing off a hard, solid object. The Air Force radar operator at Andrews backed them up."

Author Paris Flammonde, UFOs Exist!

"Studies made by the U.S. Weather Bureau . . . established beyond doubt that the targets were spurious, produced by partial trapping. Radar waves were simply being reflected by bubbles of warm air in the atmosphere."

Astrophysicist Donald H. Menzel and psychoanalyst Ernest H. Taves, *The UFO Enigma*

distances between stars are vast. If a vehicle could travel at the speed of light, 186,000 miles per second, it would take about five years to reach the nearest star. At today's rocket speed, it would take about one hundred thousand years.

However, Sachs writes, "it is conceivable that they [extraterrestrials] might have developed a method of modifying their life spans" by means of artificial hibernation.

Sachs also points out that it might be possible that extraterrestrials could use hyperspace. Hyperspace is a theoretical area of space not limited by time and normal space. If there is such a region, travel across space could happen in an instant.

In the next chapter, we'll look at some CE IIIs, encounters supposedly with real aliens. We'll see if there's any possibility that they could have overcome this problem of distance and time. For now, let's look at some of the more "earthbound" explanations.

The Washington, DC Wave

In June 1952, eight UFOs were tracked by radar by Washington National Airport. The UFOs were spotted by radar around Washington for hours. Pilots reported visuals: They were seeing strange lights in the sky.

United States Air Force jets were scrambled when UFOs were reported over Washington, DC, in July of 1952.

In July 1952, another wave of sightings occurred. F-94s were called up to investigate. One pilot, closing in on one UFO, said the light in the mysterious craft went out "like something turning off a light bulb."

Len Ortzen, author of *Strange Stories of UFOs*, says that Captain C. Pierman of Capital Airlines told reporters of lights he saw while flying over DC on July 20: "In my seventeen years of flying I've seen a lot of falling or shooting stars, but these lights were much faster than anything like that. They were about the same size as the brighter stars, and much higher than my six thousand feet. Please remember I don't speak of them as flying saucers, only very fast moving lights." What did Pierman see?

Four radar controllers at the airport agreed that nothing like an airplane could cause the blips on their scopes. Two other radar centers, one at nearby Andrews Air Force Base, called in. They had the same targets on their screens performing the same speed bursts, and the objects had moved into every square on the scopes. The objects were flying in prohibited airways over the White House and the Capitol. One

Washington National Airport radar operators are trying to determine UFO targets on a radarscope. The scoper at left is reporting their findings to officials.

of the objects was clocked at seven thousand miles per hour.

As airline pilots in the vicinity radioed that they were being followed by unknown aircraft, or that the aircraft suddenly seemed to be leaving, the blips on ground radars would appear to trail away. In the early hours after midnight, the most powerful of the radar installations located at Washington National Airport radioed the operators at Andrews that one object looked like it was hovering directly above them. Operators who rushed out to look claimed to see a huge, fiery sphere. After that, the objects vanished.

Weather Phenomena?

According to Ortzen, the Washington sightings were all blamed on weather, specifically a temperature inversion. This is a weather phenomenon which causes a mirage in the sky, and hence was the official explanation for radar and visual sightings. However, Ortzen points out that radar operators know the difference between weak blips on their screens caused by weather and strong blips caused by solid objects. Apparently they saw strong, not weak, blips, which would indicate that the sightings were more than weather mirages.

There's another UFO case explained away as being the result of natural causes. It happened at Hillsdale

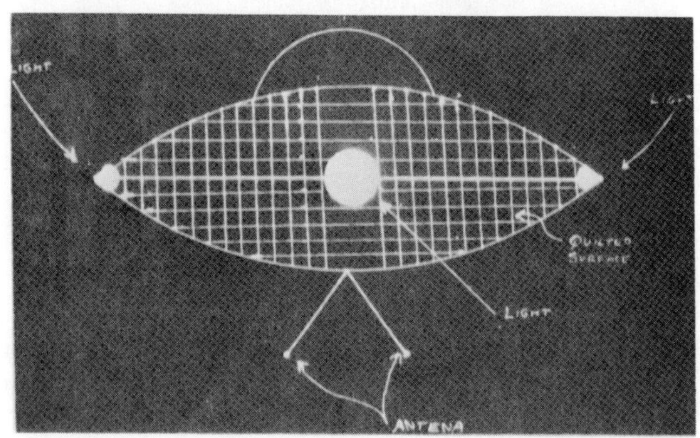

Sketch of a UFO sighted near Dexter, Michigan, by Frank Mannor and his son in 1966. It was supposed to glow and have a brown quilted surface. Mannor and his son watched it fly around the wooded swamp on his farm for thirty minutes. The next night a similar object passed over and around Hillsdale College where a number of students, a dean, and a civil defense director saw it fly for over four hours.

College in Michigan on March 20-21, 1966. UFOs were reported to be passing over nearby Milan on March 19-20. Frank Mannor and his son witnessed a glowing object rising from a swamp near their farmhouse. They called the police. En route to the scene, patrolmen saw the object fly over *them.* Mannor later described the object as being as big as a car and football-shaped. Then on March 21, at least sixty-two women students and a few adults at Hillsdale College saw a glowing object hovering over a swamp that was a few hundred yards away.

Swamp gas, will-o-the-wisp, and St. Elmo's fire are all terms for luminous occurrences which people have reported as UFOs and other oddities for years.

UFO investigator Dr. J. Allen Hynek was sent by the air force to Hillsdale to study the incident. At a press conference and under a lot of pressure to solve the mystery, he posed a possible answer: When vegetation such as that found in swamps rots, it produces swamp gas. When the gas is released, it can make popping noises and create flickering lights over marshy areas. Hynek himself wasn't truly satisfied with this explanation, but it's the one that held ground. However, many people ridiculed the idea—they said that what they saw was too vivid to be small gas eruptions.

Mass Hypnotism

Len Ortzen, in *Strange Stories of UFOs,* writes of another UFO experience:

> Probably the most famous sighting of all from the air—and there were an astonishing number reported during the 1950s from airmen of many countries—was that made by Captain James Howard of BOAC. It was also unusual in being a daytime sighting. On a June day in 1954 he was piloting an airliner from New York to London. When over the St. Lawrence estuary at 19,000 feet, with perfect visibility, he saw several flying saucers in group formation, one much larger than the others. So did the crew and stewardess and the thirty-nine passengers, and for all of twenty minutes.

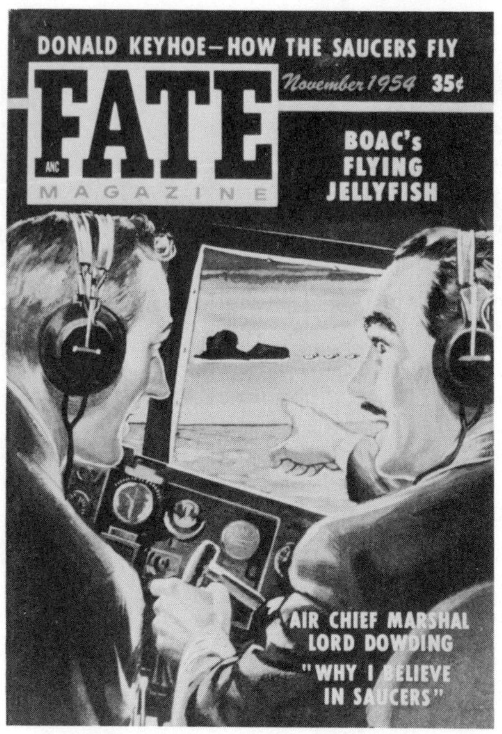

Cover of the issue of *Fate* magazine which carries the story of Captain Howard's report of UFOs.

Ortzen states that "no official explanation of this encounter was ever given. It could not be ascribed to natural phenomena or man-made objects; possibly it was a case of mass hypnotism or illusion." But who could hypnotize all those people at once, on a plane? Furthermore, Ortzen says, "a commercial flier, in particular, whose job largely depends on his emotional stability, is the last person to attempt an UFO hoax or to mistake a mirage, meteor, or satellite for a flying saucer."

Hoaxes

Are UFOs hoaxes? Apparently some are. But according to Margaret Sachs, "Only 1.66 percent of all cases studied by the United States Air Force's Project Blue Book were identified as hoaxes."

Sachs says that one of the most popular hoaxes was carried out by teenagers in the years following

Kenneth Arnold's sighting in 1947. The teenagers launched hot-air balloons that were illuminated by candles to give them a "mysterious glow." People mistook the balloons for UFOs.

Sachs further says "the most popular form of hoax seems to be the photograph. The majority of UFO photographs have been exposed as frauds."

The Socorro Case

In 1964, New Mexico policeman Lonnie Zamora said he saw a UFO land south of Socorro, New Mexico. He said he also saw two figures standing next to it, dressed in white. When they saw Zamora approach, they got back in the craft and departed.

This case has been very controversial. It illustrates that hoaxes could and do occur with UFO sightings. It was discovered after the incident that Zamora and his boss had been having financial problems. Zamora's boss owned the land adjacent to where Zamora claimed to see the UFO and its occupants. Did they make up the story for publicity purposes and for possible financial rewards?

UFO skeptic Philip Klass thinks Zamora and his boss made the story up. Zamora had claimed he saw flames coming out of the bottom of the craft as it landed and as it took off. But Klass, who studied the

Zamora cautiously approached the vehicle when flames shot out of the bottom.

landing spot, said that "there was no evidence of intense or widespread heat, or blast effects" at the site.

If not a hoax, perhaps there is another natural explanation. Klass explained the sighting with his "plasma" theory. There are four states of matter: solid, liquid, gas, and plasma. If and when a gas becomes ionized, that is, when it gains or loses electrons, then it is a plasma. On earth, plasmas occur in the upper stratosphere and when lightning strikes between thunderclouds in the lower atmosphere. Atmospheric electricity sometimes forms as ball lightning, which is lightning that is ball-shaped. Ball lightning is really a plasma and has been known to occur near high-tension wires. Such wires were near the Socorro incident.

Ronald Story says that ball lightning also has UFO characteristics: its color can be red, orange, white, blue, or yellow; its shape is usually spherical; it can glow or shine, or give off a burning appearance; by daylight it can look metallic; it can have several kinds of motions—rotating, spinning, and hovering; it can change speeds, reverse directions, roll, and float. All these characteristics sound suspiciously like descriptions of UFOs, and Klass believes this—ball lightning

A natural occurrence of ball lightning which came through a window of a hotel near Nice, France in 1902.

or other plasma phenomena—accounts for many experiences involving UFOs.

Others aren't so sure about Klass's theory. Story says that the late Dr. James E. McDonald, physicist at the University of Arizona, believed that although balls of luminosity (light) do occur, believable witnesses often seem to see UFOs as actual structural objects, not simply as lights or gases.

Other Theories

We've already encountered some theories regarding UFOs: one, that they're from other civilizations; two, they are the products of natural phenomena such as weather, visible planets, gases, balloons, plasma; three, they could be hallucinations, mirages, or optical illusions; four, they could be hoaxes. Are there other explanations?

Dr. Donald Menzel developed this diagram to offer various explanations for UFO sightings.

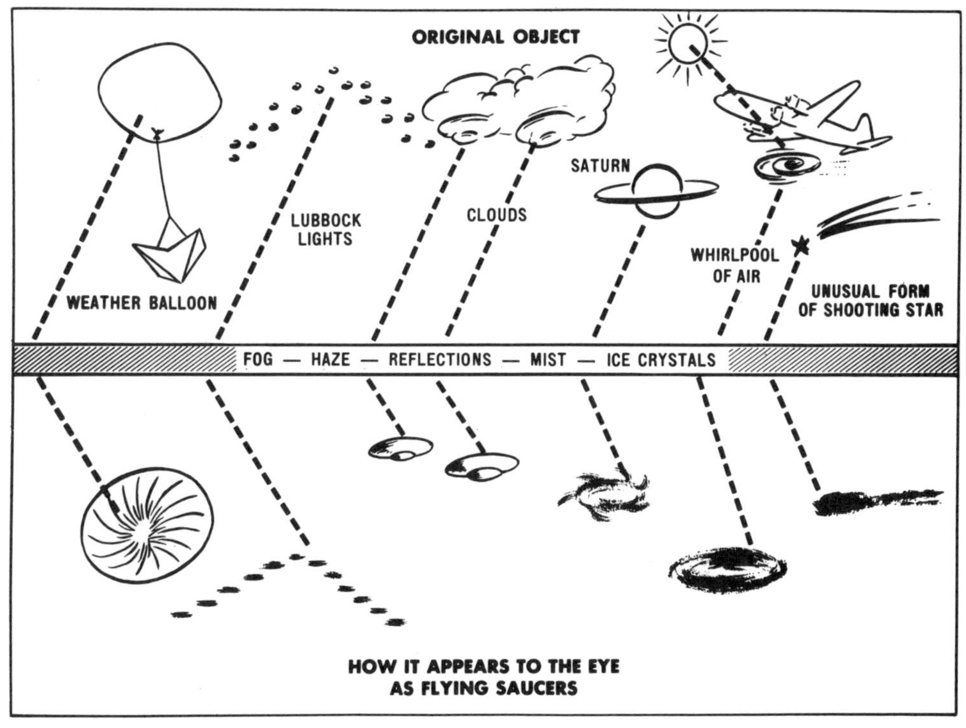

''I believe the numbers work out in such a way that UFOs as interstellar vehicles is extremely unlikely, but I think it is an equally bad mistake to say that interstellar space flight is impossible.''

Astronomer Carl Sagan, *UFOs: A Scientific Debate*

''There is no reason to believe that a spaceship, or any material thing, can travel at speeds faster than that of light.''

Astrophysicist Donald H. Menzel and psychoanalyst Ernest H. Taves, *The UFO Enigma*

Yes, and they do get far out! There's one theory that UFOs are actually space animals, living organisms!

Another is that UFOs come from underwater civilizations on earth. Writer Daniel Cohen quotes Ivan Sanderson as saying that 50 percent of all UFO sightings ''have been recorded as coming out of, going into, appearing from over, or disappearing into, water.'' Cohen admits, though, that this observation isn't startling news, as most of the earth is covered with water. Thus, it could be sheer chance that sightings occur near water and not necessarily because the theory is true.

Another theory claims that the earth is hollow and civilizations live inside it. Ray Palmer, a writer for such publications as *Amazing Stories* and one of the earliest UFO proponents, suggested in 1959 that flying saucers came and went through holes at each of the earth's poles. Scientists today, however, do not believe this.

Psychic Projection

One theory that might be credible is psychic projection. Simply stated, this means UFOs and their sightings are created by the psychic (mental) energy of the collective mind of people as a whole. That is, UFOs and their sightings are mental images projected by the minds of witnesses who think they are seeing something real.

The late psychologist Carl Jung thought such images were born out of people's psychological needs for myths to live by. We want to believe in myths. In other words, we create images of UFOs because we want to believe there are intelligent beings in the sky who can help us live and solve our problems.

Another Place and Time

Do UFOs come from another dimension? Some people think so. If it is possible that they come from a different universe through black hole travel, why couldn't there be a parallel dimension too—a place and time outside of anything we know but very similar to our own universe? UFO writer John Keel says in *UFO Operation Trojan Horse* that there could be "ultraterrestrials" who are "our next-door neighbors, part of another space-time continuum where life, matter, and energy are radically different" from, but coexisting with, ours.

George C. Andrews in *Extra-Terrestrials Among Us* suggests this might be why UFO sightings have occurred in abundance since the early days of atomic bombs. Perhaps, if aliens have parallel dimensions within our own time and space, they, too, are concerned about nuclear war. The power of our wars would affect their dimensions as well!

Here's what Andrews writes: "UFOs share the same space with us, as they operate outside our normal range of frequencies, interacting only when they wish to. A nuclear bomb is a miniature sun, which emits energy on all spectrums, not just the Earth range of frequencies that humans are sensitive to. Therefore nuclear war would annihilate not only terrestrial humanity, but also many forms of intelligent life inhabiting dimensions we normally have no awareness of or contact with. So no wonder we are being visited by aliens."

UFO photograph taken by George J. Stock over Passaic, New Jersey, in August of 1952.

Do UFOs come from another time? Are they time travelers? It is a possibility. Scientifically speaking, it is assumed that someday humanity might be able to manipulate time as well as space. We might be able to travel into the past and into the future. Ronald Story has suggested that UFOs might be visiting their own past (us and our present time) but do not want to interfere with our affairs. They just come to see how we are doing. Could it be that we are the aliens' past?

Daniel Cohen, in his book *The Ancient Visitors,* comments on the possibility of aliens traveling to us from the future: "UFOs from the future would clear up a lot of problems. . . . It would explain why the creatures that are often described as piloting the craft usually look so human." They are often described as looking very different from us but with many of the same basic human characteristics—two arms and legs, eyes, mouth, etc. We do not exactly look like our Neanderthal and other ancestors—why should our descendants look just like us?

Cohen adds, "It would explain why these visitors are so interested in what we are doing. . . .We might be of great interest to our descendants, but would we be interesting enough to strangers for them to repeatedly travel light years to check upon how we are getting along?"

Stephen Pratt saw these unidentified flying objects over South Yorkshire in England on March 28, 1966. Is alien intelligent life trying to contact us to warn us not to destroy ourselves with atom bombs?

Although Cohen entertains some fascinating questions, he is skeptical of the idea of aliens from the future. "Such speculations have already served as the basis for countless science fiction tales. That is the realm for which they are best suited."

Physical Evidence

Aside from UFO sightings, is there any evidence to show that UFOs, as genuine alien spacecraft, exist? Let's consider a few examples in which it was, for a time, believed real evidence was found.

Ronald Story in *UFOs and the Limits of Science* writes of some famous and controversial evidence that was found in Sao Paulo, Brazil, in the 1960s. Three metallic fragments supposedly from a UFO were mailed to the Rio de Janeiro newspaper, *O Globo,* addressed to reporter Ibrahim Sued. A mysterious letter included with the fragments said the pieces were from a "flying disk" that had exploded. Here is the letter:

Men in Toulouse, France, drew on the side of a barn a figure they said they saw step out of a mysterious spherical ship. They described a "small-sized man" wearing an outfit like a deep-sea diver. This is another example of a human-looking alien with two large eyes.

Dear Mr. Ibrahim Sued. As a faithful reader of your column, and an admirer of yours, I wish to give you something of the highest interest to a newspaperman, concerning the flying saucers. If you believe they are real, of course. I also didn't believe anything said or published about them. But just a few days ago I had to change my mind. I was fishing together with some friends at a place near the town of Ubatuba, Sao Paulo, when I saw a flying disk. It approached the beach at unbelievable speed, an accident seeming imminent—in other words, a crash into the sea. . . . At the last moment, however, when it was about to strike the water, it made a sharp turn upwards and climbed up rapidly in a fantastic maneuver. We followed the spectacle with our eyes, startled, when we saw the disk explode in flames. It disintegrated into thousands of fiery fragments, which fell sparkling with magnificent brightness. They looked like fireworks, in spite of the time of the accident—at noon. Most of these fragments, almost all, fell into the sea. But a number of small pieces fell close to the beach and we picked up a large amount of this material—which was light as paper. I enclose herewith a small sample of it. I don't know anyone that could be trusted to whom I might send

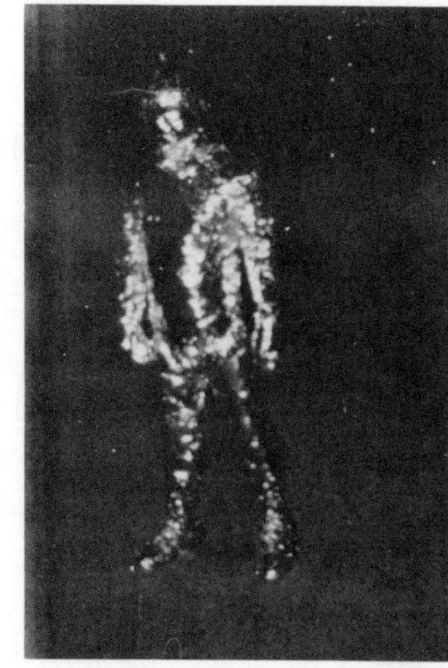

Two pictures taken of a strange-looking creature by a policeman in Falkville, Alabama in October of 1973. This looks like a typical hoax photo of an alien in a strange metallic suit.

> it for analysis. I never read about a flying saucer having been found, or about fragments or parts of a saucer that had been picked up; unless it had been done by military authorities and the whole thing kept as a top-secret subject.

Unfortunately, because the letter's signature was unreadable and there was no return address, whoever wrote the letter couldn't be contacted for further information. Hence the big question: Were the fragments real and the letter true, or was it all a hoax?

The metallic samples were tested by several scientists. However the results were contradictory and puzzling. Dr. Olavo T. Fontes of Brazil took the metallic samples for the first tests. One sample tested by Fortes seemed to be an ultra-pure piece of magnesium. But other samples tested in 1967 at the University of Colorado didn't seem quite so pure. Of those results, Dr. Roy Craig said, "The claim of unusual purity of the magnesium fragments has been disproved. The fragments do not show unique or unearthly composition, and therefore they cannot be used as valid evidence of the extraterrestrial origin of a vehicle of which they are claimed to have been a part."

"I don't talk about UFOs very much anymore, I talk about the UFO *phenomenon*. . . . The phenomenon is the continual flow of reports, now from 140 countries—and our databank now has over 100,000 entries."

Astronomer and UFO researcher J. Allen Hynek, *The Search for Extraterrestrial Intelligence*

"I maintain that we have found the answer to the question 'What are UFOs?' . . . Our answer must be that UFOs do not exist."

Skeptical investigator of UFOs Robert Sheaffer, *The UFO Verdict: Examining the Evidence*

Strange Results from Tests

Yet, in another test in 1969, Dr. Walter W. Walker, professor of metallurgical engineering at the University of Arizona, did a structural analysis of the sample. He found an unusual thing: All the grains, or crystals, of the metal were aligned in a single direction. This phenomenon is called *directional solidification.* Walker, in an interview with Ronald Story, said, "This might be interpreted as meaning that the samples were from a more advanced culture." He also said, "To my knowledge, no commercially pure magnesium is used in *any* vehicle" that we presently have on earth.

Was there an alien spacecraft that crashed in Brazil? There is no absolute agreement. The ultimate judgment? The evidence is inconclusive!

What, after all, would unquestionable evidence consist of? Dr. Dave Williams, NASA space administrator, answers: "Give me one little green man—not a theory or memory of one."

Some people claim that extraterrestrials *have* been found. For example, Frank Scully, in *Behind the Flying Saucers,* claimed that a crashed spacecraft had once been investigated by the U.S. In Scully's story, thirty-four alien bodies were pulled from the wreck. They were humanoids between thirty-six and forty-two inches tall. Scully's informant about the crash was a friend, Silas M. Newton, who got his information from a mysterious Dr. Gee. Subsequently, the entire story was proven to be a hoax in 1952.

From time to time other reports pop up about crashed UFOs and of dead or alive aliens. Most often these appear in grocery store tabloids. There have even been claims that an alien was kept alive for study for several years at a secret military base. But these stories always turn out to be tall tales. No one has ever publicly proven that an alien has ever been found.

This is a typical UFO occupant, a "Little Green Man." This drawing is based on 300 cases of sightings.

Even without genuine aliens, many other claims of UFO evidence have been made. A common report is that UFOs create a substance called angel's hair. It looks like fine strands of hair or spun-glass wool. Witnesses report that it is a cobweblike material that appears to fall from the sky and usually evaporates immediately after being touched.

Ufologist Raymond Fowler reported that angel's hair fell on October 15, 1952, in Oloron, France:

> At 12:50 p.m., a huge white cylindrical object tilted at a 45 degree angle moved silently across the skies accompanied by about 30 domed disks travelling in pairs. Electric-like flashes arced between each pair. . . . Wispy filaments of material fell to the ground in large amounts where it evaporated into nothingness.

Story also informs us that a sample of angel's hair, retrieved from a fall in San Francisco on October 11, 1977, was analyzed by Dr. Joseph S. Accetta of the Los Alamos Scientific Laboratory in New Mexico. The results showed that the substance was a spider web! This isn't surprising—it is known that spiders can migrate through the sky by spinning out strands of web and then riding them. This is called ballooning. Fowler also found that spider migratory seasons are

Author and investigator Raymond Fowler.

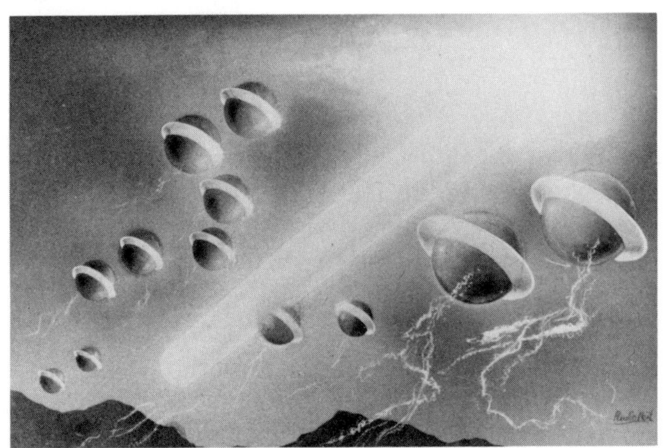

Sighting at Olorons, St. Marie, France.

"The least improbable explanation is that these things [UFOs] are artificial and controlled. . . . My opinion for some time has been that they have extraterrestrial origin."

Aerodynamicist and mathematical physicist Maurice Bilot, *Life*, April 7, 1952

"In every case which I have personally investigated, the 'UFO' sighting turns out to have been a media exaggeration, misunderstanding, distortion, or outright fabrication."

Author James E. Oberg, *UFOs & Outer Space Mysteries*

in the spring and fall, and he said that 80 percent of the UFO sightings involving angel's hair were reported in the month of October: fall time.

Blobs

Another mysterious piece of physical evidence reported to come from UFOs are "blobs," usually seen on lawns or falling out of the sky. Blobs? Wasn't that the name of an old movie? Is this for real?

Ronald Story tells of a blob being found. He writes that two police officers on patrol in Philadelphia on September 26, 1950, "saw the object fall into a field, so they parked their car and got out to investigate. What they found was an object about six feet in diameter, about one foot thick at the center, and a couple of inches thick at the edge. . . . It quivered as though it were alive and gave off a purplish glow."

In another instance, three purple blobs fell into the yard of a Mr. and Mrs. Christian in Frisco, Texas. It was a jellylike substance with bits of lead in it. Did these blobs come from UFOs? Not according to Ron DiIulio, assistant director of the Fort Worth Museum of Science and History. While visiting a battery-reprocessing plant in Frisco, he found a garbage area that contained heaps of similar blobs. DiIulio thought that these were the mysterious blobs being found in people's yards. Chemical tests performed at NASA backed up DiIulio's claim that the blobs were of an industrial origin, not extraterrestrial.

Photographs

Books on UFOs and newspapers sometimes contain photographs of UFOs that are quite realistic. However, most of them have been proven to be fake. Ronald Story says that most are worthless as evidence for these reasons: The imagery is usually so poor that they give no meaningful information; some vital element is missing (such as the original negative, which can be analyzed for fraud); testimony doesn't match the photograph (for example, maybe a witness

Is this a picture of a hovering UFO? No, it is a metal plate tossed into the air by the photographer. Some photos are as simple as this to explain; others are much more complicated.

says he or she saw two UFOs, but the photograph shows only one); there are inconsistencies within the photograph, such as a double exposure (indicating that the negative has been exposed twice—which could mean that someone has tinkered with the film to create a fake).

Hoaxes Explained

Len Ortzen tells what most fakes are really pictures of: lampshades, garbage can lids, soup plates, model UFOs, motorized toy airplanes, and marks or smudges on the negative.

Donald Menzel and Ernest Taves cite an example of a hoax that was figured out by UFO skeptic James Oberg. This involves a UFO seen and photographed from space by NASA spacecraft *Gemini 7.* The photograph apparently showed two glowing objects with force fields around them. Oberg found that the real photo had been touched up by someone to make it appear that the sun's glare reflecting off two rocket thrusters was two UFOs.

Menzel and Taves also cite an example of two photographs taken of UFOs by a pair of teenage boys. The photos were investigated by the Condon Com-

UFO sightings happen all over the world. This picture was taken by a young boy in Malaga, Spain, in January of 1984.

mittee, a group affiliated with the air force investigation of UFOs. According to Menzel and Taves, the two boys

> said they had seen from their suburban backyard a disk-like object hovering in the sky. They took a Polaroid photo of the object, which then began to move away. As quickly as possible—about eight seconds later—they took a second picture.
>
> The Colorado [Condon] investigator studied the photographs and found that during the alleged eight-second interval there had been gross [huge] changes in cloud structure and position that could not have occurred in that short time.''
>
> Conclusion: The photos were a hoax.

Beyond all the sightings, the assumed physical evidence, and the photographs, what else is there to the mystery of UFOs? Plenty, as we'll see.

Project Blue Book

As a result of continued sightings, the U.S. government feared a foreign country truly might be testing new weapons that could threaten national security. Therefore, the U.S. Air Force initiated a program to investigate the UFO phenomenon.

It began as Project Sign in 1947. Author Brad Steiger says Project Sign evaluated 243 UFO reports in its two years. It concluded that ''No definite and conclusive evidence is yet available that would prove or disprove the existence of these UFOs as real aircraft of unknown and unconventional configurations.''

But the air force continued investigating. Project Sign became Project Grudge, so named because it took a negative attitude toward the study of UFOs.

In 1951, Project Grudge became Project Blue Book. It was based at Wright-Patterson Air Force Base in Dayton, Ohio. Headed by Captain Edward J. Ruppelt, Project Blue Book investigated, to one degree or another, over 10,000 reports of UFO sightings. Of these, 701 remained unidentified.

In the mid-1960s, the air force's involvement with UFO studies reached a climax. The press and some members of Congress accused the air force of secrecy and incompetence regarding its UFO investigation. Consequently, the University of Colorado was contracted to undergo an independent two-year study of UFOs.

In 1969, the university released its *Condon Report*, which recommended that Project Blue Book be closed. Secretary of the Air Force Robert C. Seamans Jr. announced the termination of the project, stating

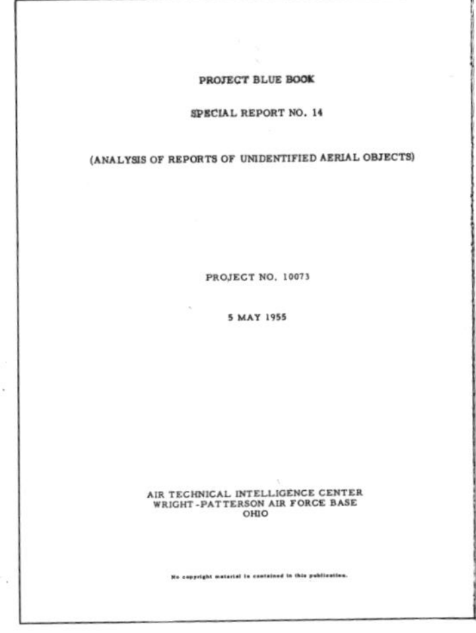

PROJECT BLUE BOOK

SPECIAL REPORT NO. 14

(ANALYSIS OF REPORTS OF UNIDENTIFIED AERIAL OBJECTS)

PROJECT NO. 10073

5 MAY 1955

AIR TECHNICAL INTELLIGENCE CENTER
WRIGHT-PATTERSON AIR FORCE BASE
OHIO

No copyright material is contained in this publication.

This is the cover page of the air force's *Special Report No. 14*. The manuscript compiled reports, analyzed the data, and summarized its findings: ''Therefore . . . it is considered to be highly improbable that reports of unidentified aerial objects examined in this study represent observations of technological developments outside of the range of present-day scientific knowledge. It is emphasized that there has been a complete lack of any valid evidence of physical matter in any case of a reported unidentified aerial object.''

Seated at the desk is Major Hector Quintanilla, who became the last director of the air force Project Blue Book. The project was established to investigate reports of unidentified flying objects.

Dr. J. Allen Hynek, astronomer and Project Blue Book consultant, has investigated unidentified flying objects since the 1940s.

that it could no longer "be justified either on the ground of national security or in the interest of science." Officials believed that UFO reports simply didn't warrant further study.

However, Dr. J. Allen Hynek disagreed. As a consultant for the air force for twenty years, he reviewed UFO reports. He believed the air force had mishandled its investigations. They had falsely assumed that reports of UFOs were not to be taken seriously. In his book, *The UFO Experience: A Scientific Inquiry,* Hynek writes:

> I have had an opportunity to read and study *all* the reports in the Blue Book files, to interview many hundreds of witnesses—the reporters of UFO experiences—and even to testify several times before congressional groups.
>
> Thus, I became aware of some very interesting cases, most of which were submerged in a veritable quagmire of nonsense reports.

Inadequate Investigations

Hynek says UFOs were inadequately investigated during Project Sign; the air force adopted a brush-off attitude toward UFOs during Project Grudge; and on Project Blue Book, Hynek says, "only the most [indifferent] attempts were made to mount any type of serious investigations. This was especially true of the particularly puzzling, unusual cases."

Hynek quotes from a vivid report in the Project Blue Book files that was never followed up. This occurred on August 1, 1965.

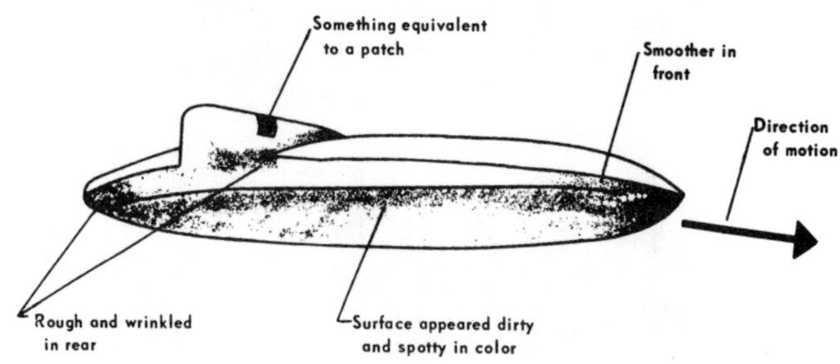

One of thousands of reports Project Blue Book received, this Case X sketch of a sighting on May 24, 1949, was made by employees of an aeronautical laboratory in Oregon. They claimed the object reflected sunlight, was metallic, and moved horizontally, picking up speed rapidly but with no apparent means of propulsion. Observation time was two-and-a-half to three minutes.

2:50 a.m.—Nine more UFOs were sighted, and at 3:35 a.m. Colonel Williams, Commanding Officer of the Sioux Army Depot, at Sydney, Nebraska, reported five UFOs going east.

4:40 a.m.—Captain Howell, Air Force Command Post, called Dayton and Defense Intelligence Agency to report that a Strategic Air Command Team at site H-2 at 3:00 a.m. reported a white oval UFO directly overhead. Later Strategic Air Command Post passed the following: Francis W. Warren Air Force Base reports (Site B-4 3:17 a.m.)—a UFO 90 miles east of Cheyenne at a high rate of speed and descending—oval and white with white lines on its sides and a flashing red light in its center moving east; reported to have landed 10 miles east of the site.

When Hynek asked what was being done about investigating the report, he was told by Major Quintanilla, the officer in charge, that the sightings were stars.

Was the air force's decision to terminate Project Blue Book right? Hynek's observations seem to indicate that there is much more to the UFO mystery than the air force was willing to admit.

As a result of the air force investigations, some scientists decided to further pursue the UFO question by themselves. J. Allen Hynek and Jacques Vallee were among the founders of CUFOS, the Center for UFO Studies, located in Lima, Ohio. Created in 1973, it was the first group devoted to scientific research on UFOs. Other groups formed later.

There is no clear agreement on whether UFOs are science fiction or science fact. Many people, however, have claimed to experience UFOs firsthand. Are their accounts to be believed?

This photo was part of a series taken through the window of a truck. Is it a hoax? The picture was sent to the National Investigation Committee on Aerial Phenomena at the University of Colorado by Rex Heflin in March of 1967. Investigators found that by hanging a camera lens cap just a few inches outside the truck window a very similar picture is produced.

Four

Have UFOs Really Kidnapped People?

UFO sightings have been reported by the thousands. They almost seem common. Yet there is another kind of UFO experience, even more puzzling—abduction by aliens. Have some present-day people actually been taken aboard UFOs as they claim? Why would UFOs want to abduct humans? In this chapter, we'll look at three important cases of supposed UFO abductions. What happens in an abduction? UFO investigator and author D. Scott Rogo, editor of *Alien Abductions: True Cases of UFO Kidnappings,* says that many abductions follow a pattern:

> The witness will be driving along some lonely and deserted area when he becomes aware of a UFO, either following his car or hovering at the side of the road. This is usually all the witness will consciously remember. After making his initial observation, he will often "black out" and will only come to about an hour or so later with no conscious memory of what has taken place during the interim. In the following weeks, though, he may begin to realize that something extraordinary has happened to him. He may start having dreams of a UFO abduction, or develop odd obsessions and compulsions. These stressful developments will eventually encourage him to seek help from a ufologist [a UFO investigator], or perhaps

A Texas sheriff and his deputy search the night sky for a reported flying saucer.

a psychiatrist; and these professionals will usually suggest hypnotic regression . . . back to the scene of the encounter which helps the witness remember exactly what happened to him. Under hypnosis, [the person is asked to regress, or go back, to sometime in the past] the victim will invariably recall how he stopped his car after seeing the UFO and watched helplessly as alien beings came out of the craft and forced him into it. He will go on to describe how he was subjected to a medical examination or shown a series of visions before being returned to his car—with the admonition that he forget all that had transpired. After his encounter and his recollection of the event, the witness might also experience further mental contacts or even visitations by UFO entities for years to come. Often they will appear right in his home through a process of materialization.

Betty and Barney Hill

The first fully documented case of an abduction was reported in John Fuller's book *The Interrupted Journey,* published in 1966. Fuller, an investigative

Social workers Betty and Barney Hill with a copy of John Fuller's book about their experience.

reporter, tells the story of Betty and Barney Hill's experience on September 19, 1961. Briefly, here is that story.

The Hills and their dachshund, Delsey, were returning home from a vacation in Canada, through Niagara Falls. Driving through the White Mountains of New Hampshire, they were headed for their home in Portsmouth, New Hampshire. It was about nine in the evening and U.S. Highway 3 was deserted. The moon was bright. Betty saw a light in the sky that seemed to grow larger and approach their car. Betty noted the bright object was moving. They got out their binoculars for a look. Barney thought the object was probably a star or a satellite, but Betty was convinced it was something else. Perhaps an airplane, Barney thought.

They drove on, but stopped around eleven o'clock near Cannon Mountain to look at the object. It swung from a northern flight pattern toward the west, made its turn, and headed back toward the Hills. Betty was certain the object was following them. Barney, reaching for explanations, then said it might be a Piper Cub or a helicopter. But through the binoculars he saw a shape that seemed to have a series of blinking lights along the fuselage. They flashed red, amber, green, and blue.

Followed by a UFO

They got back into their car and continued to drive toward Cannon Mountain at a little more than five miles per hour. The object followed, moving erratically in the sky. They drove past a motel. The object now appeared huge and was only a few hundred feet above the ground. Its lights changed from blinking colors to a steady white glow.

Their 1957 Chevrolet Bel Air was vibrating. Betty looked through the binoculars again. She saw, clearly, a double row of windows on the object. "Barney, you've got to *stop*. You've never seen anything like this in your life," Betty said.

"The conclusion is inescapable: no unusual object was present. What Mrs. Hill was calling a 'UFO' was in fact the brilliant planet Jupiter."

Author and UFO skeptic Robert Sheaffer, *The UFO Verdict: Examining the Evidence*

"We knew we had seen a craft, a solid metal object. There was no escaping that."

Betty Hill, quoted in *Direct Encounters: Personal Histories of UFO Abductees*

Chevrolet

Barney stopped the car. He got out to look with the binoculars. The object swung toward them. Barney described it later as being as wide in diameter as the distance between three telephone poles. He found himself walking toward it across a field. The huge object was shaped like a pancake. Scared, Betty screamed for Barney to come back to the car. He kept walking.

Barney stopped in the field, and, through the binoculars, he could see at least six figures behind the windows, staring at him. They were wearing uniforms. The craft started to land. Fins projected out from its sides along with red lights. Barney focused on one of the figures in the craft. It was staring at him. Barney had never seen eyes like that. Terrified, he ran back to the car.

Betty was nearly hysterical.

Barney sped down the road. Both of them heard a beeping sound from the rear of the car. They became drowsy, and a haze seemed to envelop them.

Opposite page:
An artist's drawing of the Hills stopping to look at the strange lights following them.

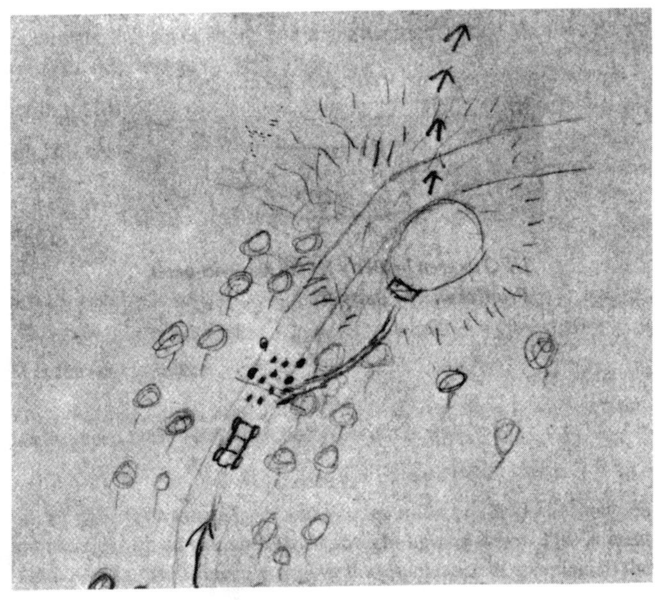

This picture was drawn by Barney after he went through therapy to try to understand what happened. This is his recollection of the site of the abduction. The dots represent "men in the road" and the round object in the clearing notes his remembrance of the position of the ship.

Under hypnosis Barney drew a simple picture of the leader of his abductors. After listening to a tape recording of his own account, he went into a trance and drew a second sketch. He said their eyes were elongated and their lips had no muscles.

Later, down the road, they returned to full consciousness. They had driven thirty-five miles and could not remember the last two hours. They arrived home at five in the morning. They had expected to get there by three at the latest.

The next day, Betty found shiny white spots on the trunk of the car. She waved a compass over the trunk. Its needle wavered and spun around.

After the incident, Betty experienced recurring nightmares and anxiety. Barney experienced health problems. His ulcers flared up. They sought psychiatric help. They were hypnotized. During a session, they revealed their experience. According to documented records, they claimed to have been taken aboard a UFO. They had been examined by alien creatures. Betty also revealed that the aliens had showed her a star map showing the aliens' homeland.

Controversy About the Hills' Story

Were the Hills really whisked aboard a spacecraft? Examined? Shown a map?

UFO investigator Robert Sheaffer in his book *The UFO Verdict* writes that the UFO the Hills saw was actually the planet Jupiter. But how would that account for the object moving and following the Hills' car?

What about the star map that resembled the constellation Zeta Reticuli? Daniel Cohen, in *The World of UFOs*, says that Betty's map *"doesn't* exactly match the arrangement of any known group of stars, not without some fudging, ignoring one feature and emphasizing another." UFO critic James Oberg suggests in his book *UFOs and Outer Space Mysteries* that "any random set of dots and lines can be matched to the randomly strewn stars in the solar 'neighborhood' out to twenty or thirty light years."

Dr. Benjamin Simon, the psychiatrist who treated the Hills, is quoted by John Fuller in *The Interrupted Journey* as saying, "The story was quite improbable on the basis of any existing scientific data, but on the other hand it appeared as the case went on that the Hills were not lying, and I felt convinced of that." However, he further says, "I was ultimately left with the conclusion" that the best explanation of Mrs. Hill's strange experiences and dreams was "the aftermath of some type of experience with an Unidentified Flying Object or some[thing] similar [and that it] assumed the quality of a fantasized experience."

Were the Hills kidnapped? No one knows for certain. Betty claimed that while she was on the ship, a long needle had been inserted into her navel for a pregnancy test. This sounds familiar. Other abductees have claimed this same kind of incident. Could this be a part of a UFO pattern?

Sketch by Barney Hill showing the figures, fins, and red lights.

Fuller points out several facts about the case that he says cannot be argued. First, a sighting of some sort took place. Second, the object sighted appears to have been a craft. Third, the sighting caused a severe emotional reaction. Fourth, personal anxieties of the Hills intensified the emotional response to the sighting. Fifth, the Hills had no ulterior motive to create such a story. Sixth, the case was investigated by several technical and scientific persons who support the possibility that the experience was real. Seventh, there is a measurable amount of direct physical circumstantial evidence—for example, the shiny spots on the car, and the behavior of Betty's compass—to support the experience. And eighth, under hypnosis, the Hills told almost identical stories concerning what happened during the two hours they could not remember.

The Andreasson Case

Another famous abduction case resembles not only the Hills' experience but also fits Rogo's description of abduction patterns. This case includes a mysterious light, amnesia, memories of an abduction, and the use of hypnosis to help the abductee to recover, or remember, what happened during the amnesia period.

Becky Andreasson (Betty's daughter) also agreed to undergo hypnosis in an effort to remember exactly what happened.

According to D. Scott Rogo, it happened on the night of January 25, 1967, in the country home of Mrs. Betty Andreasson and her family. It was a winter night, cold and snowy. Most of Mrs. Andreasson's seven children and their grandfather were watching television in the living room when the whole area became quiet and the house lights started flickering, then went out. The family rushed to the kitchen. A pink light shone through the kitchen window.

Waino Aho, Mrs. Andreasson's immigrant Finnish father, first saw the creatures through the pantry window. He described them later as "Halloween freaks." Small, they hopped like grasshoppers outside the house. Aho returned to the living room with the rest of the family, where they all found themselves to be in a sort of suspended animation. When they finally snapped out of it, a considerable length of time had passed.

Over the next few months, Betty and her daughter Becky slowly remembered that aliens had entered their home that winter night in 1967. In 1977, Betty and Becky underwent a series of hypnotic sessions to help them find out what had happened.

Mrs. Andreasson remembered that the aliens had materialized in the house through a closed door. They "came in like follow-the-leader . . . right through the wood, one right after the other." They walked through it like ghosts. Raymond Fowler, author of *The Andreasson Affair,* quotes Betty's description of them:

> They were identical, except the leader, who appeared taller. The creatures had gray skins, large, out-

Betty Andreasson, under hypnosis, recalls the fear and pain of her abduction. Joseph Santangelo, UFO investigator with the Mutual UFO Network, tapes her memories.

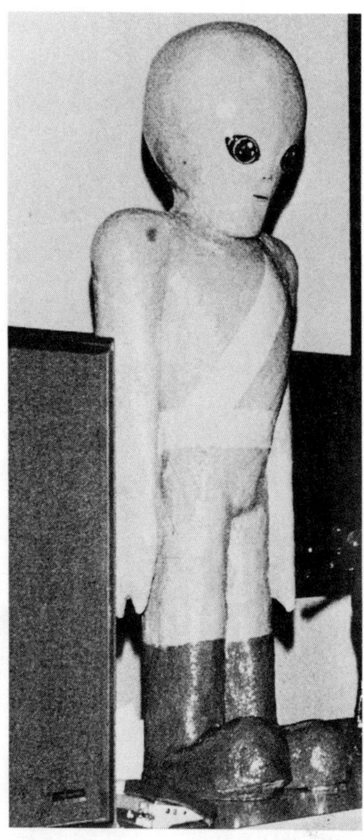

A model of Quazgaa, leader of the entities in Betty Andreasson's UFO abduction case.

> sized pear-shaped heads. Their faces were mongoloid in appearance. . . . They wore shiny dark blue, form-fitting uniforms. Each sleeve was adorned with an emblem that resembled a bird with outstretched wings. Their three-digited hands were gloved, and they wore high shoes or boots.

They seemed to be friendly and they telepathically communicated with Betty Andreasson.

Betty says she was "floated" to the UFO craft by the aliens. While in the craft, Betty Andreasson had both physical and supernatural experiences. She underwent a medical examination in a dome-shaped, rounded room. A long silver needle was inserted not only into her navel, but also up her left nostril and into her head. She remembered traveling into a mysterious environment where she had visions of buildings that looked like pyramids, distant cities, a green sky, bright lights that reflected off "crystalline structures," and a particularly memorable one of a huge phoenix—a legendary bird—being consumed and reborn as a worm. Before she was returned to her home, Mrs. Andreasson was told she must forget what had occurred during her abduction.

According to D. Scott Rogo, Mrs. Andreasson had another visitation experience several years after her initial one. She was lying in bed late one night with her husband and heard someone moving in the room. She turned her head and witnessed a being made of light. It was four or five feet tall, but it did not seem to have material substance. When the creature realized it had been noticed, it ran downstairs and disappeared. Did Mrs. Andreasson see an alien?

Abduction in Brazil

Reports of abductions do not just come from the U.S. They also are reported in other countries. A fascinating case occurred on a family farm near the town of Francisco de Sales in Sao Paulo, Brazil, on October 5, 1957.

According to his deposition, given to Dr. Olvao T. Fontes on February 22, 1980, Antonio Villas-Boas, a twenty-three-year-old farmer, was in his room with his brother at about 11:00 p.m. He opened the windows for some cool air. "Then I saw, right in the middle of the yard, a silvery fluorescent reflection, brighter than moonlight, lighting up the whole ground," said Villas-Boas. The light came toward the house, over the roof and shined through the tiles. Then it went out.

On October 14, an episode occurred again around 9:30 to 10:00 p.m. Villas-Boas and his brother were on a tractor, plowing a field. Suddenly they saw a "very bright light" that was stationary on the northern end of the field. It was "big and round" and "seemed to be a hundred meters" off the ground. It was light red. Villas-Boas walked toward the object twenty times. Each time it would maneuver itself away. He grew tired of chasing it and walked back to his brother. The light suddenly vanished.

The next day, October 15, Villas-Boas was plowing the same field. This time he was alone. It was late

"Under hypnosis, Betty Andreasson and her daughter relived a consistent, detailed UFO experience with genuine psychological reactions."

Author Raymond E. Fowler, *The Andreasson Affair*

"Betty Andreasson's experience aboard the spaceship, and especially after the examination, are very much like experiences reported under the influence of LSD."

Mutual UFO Network researcher Willard D. Nelson, from his paper *A Viewpoint on the Andreasson Affair*

The scene looked something like this when Villas-Boas said aliens set their craft down in his fields.

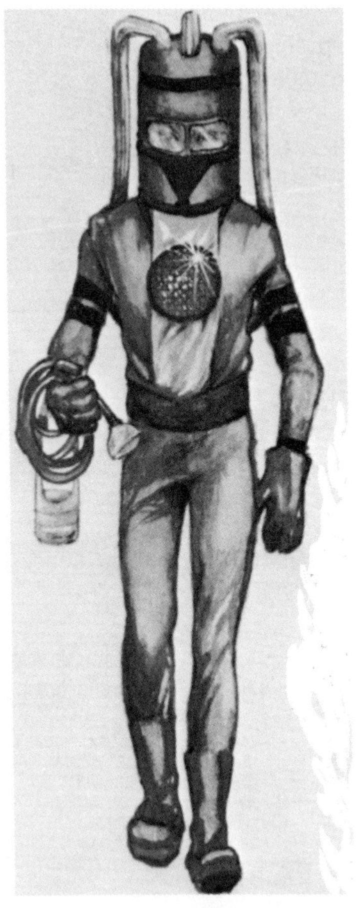

Villas-Boas described the beings who took him aboard their ship as wearing tight overalls connected to their helmets by three silvery tubes. The suits each had a pineapple-sized red shield on the chest.

at night, about 1:00 a.m. The sky was clear and covered with stars. Suddenly, he saw what he thought was a red star. However, he realized it was not a star for it grew larger. It moved in his direction.

"In a few moments it had grown into a very luminous, egg-shaped object, flying towards me at a terrific speed." Then it stationed itself about fifty meters above his head, lighting up the tractor and the ground around it. Villas-Boas started his tractor and tried to escape, but the tractor's engine and its lights suddenly died. He jumped off and started to run. Then something grabbed him.

The Abduction

"My pursuer was a short individual (reaching to my shoulders) and dressed in strange clothing," he said. He struggled with the being until he was overcome by three more of the strange assailants. They dragged him into the craft. He was taken to a room. They undressed him and sponged him. They took a blood sample from his chin.

Villas-Boas describes the men as being dressed in "very tight-fitting overalls." Their eyes appeared smaller than human eyes and appeared to be blue. Their clothing appeared to be uniforms.

Shortly after, a beautiful, naked woman entered. She had large, blue, slanted eyes. "Her nose was straight, without being pointed, nor turned up, nor too big. What was different was the contour of her face, for the cheekbones were very high, making the face very wide (much wider than in the South American Indian woman). But then, immediately below, the face narrowed very sharply, terminating in a pointed chin. This feature gave the lower half of her face a quite triangular shape."

Villas-Boas claimed the woman had sex with him. Then, when she was leaving the room, she pointed to her belly, to Villas-Boas, and to the sky. Subsequently, Villas-Boas was escorted off the craft, which then rose into the air. Suddenly, at a great speed, it vanished to the south.

This case presents a different abduction pattern. Villas-Boas was abducted while fully conscious. This kind of abduction has been reported in other cases. What's unusual about this case is that a sexual encounter occurred between an alien and a human.

Why Are UFOs Interested in Humans?

Was Villas-Boas really chased down by a UFO and its occupants? Why was he, like the Hills and Mrs. Betty Andreasson, taken aboard? Why did the aliens want to mate with a human? Many of those who claim to have been abducted say the aliens were interested in their reproductive organs. Why so much interest

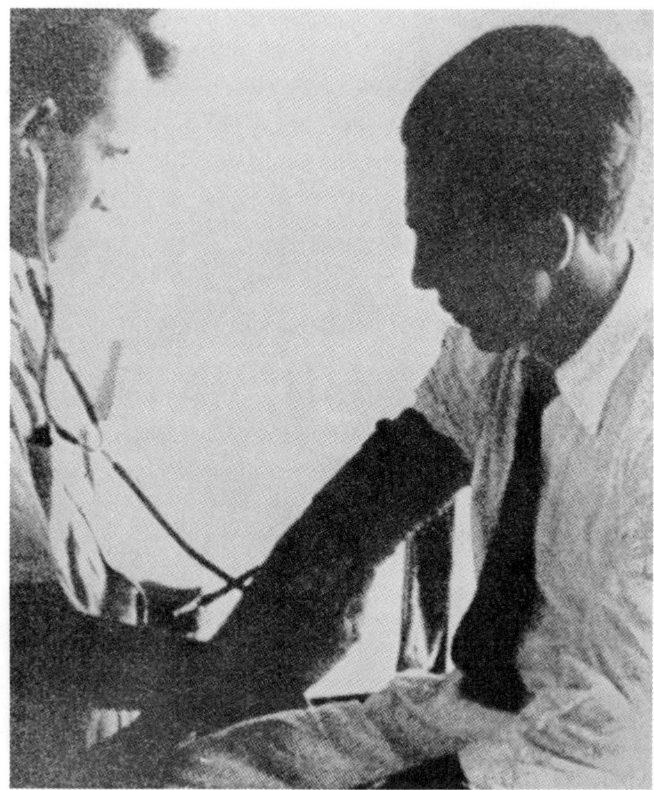

Antonio Villas-Boas is medically examined after he claimed he was abducted by aliens aboard a UFO in Brazil in October of 1957.

"Ages ago an unknown space-ship found out that the earth had all the prerequisites for intelligent life to develop. . . . The spacemen artificially fertilised some female members . . . and departed."

Author Erich von Däniken, *Chariots of the Gods?*

"No evidence has so far been presented supporting the hypothesis of man's partial or total extraterrestrial origin which survives critical scrutiny."

Author Ronald Story, *Guardians of the Universe?*

in reproduction? Budd Hopkins, author of *Intruders, The Incredible Visitations at Copley Woods*, speculates that "somewhere, somehow, human beings—or possibly hybrids of some sort—are being produced by a technology . . . superior to ours."

D. Scott Rogo in *Alien Abductions* quotes Ann Druffel as saying, "UFO entities seem interested in man's evolution and his procreative abilities. Without reproduction, nothing can evolve. UFOs seem to be looking after man's continuing evolution." Why? Are they also human? Are they ensuring the continuance of the human race? Are we to believe the human race is undergoing genetic experiments by aliens?

What about experiments that may have occurred in the past? Was Neanderthal man a failed experiment that gave rise to Cro-Magnon man—our ancestors? Could it be that genetic experiments going on now will give rise to the next stage of human development? These are interesting questions, but no one can answer them for certain, one way or another.

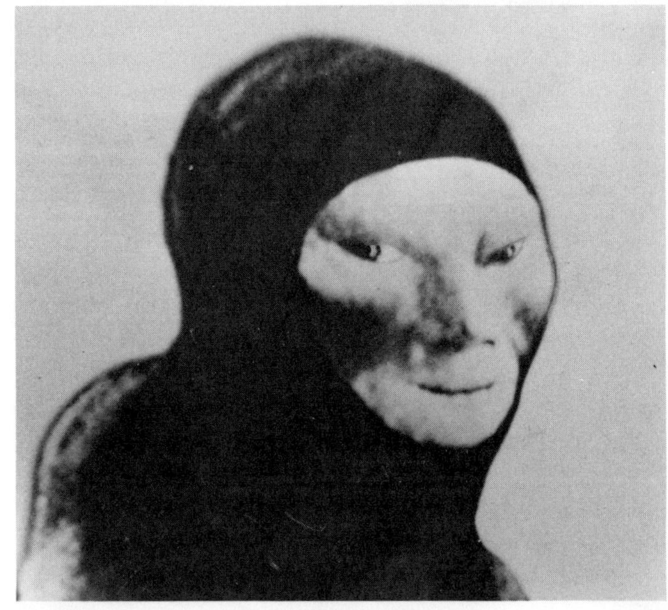

On May 10, 1978, in Emilcin, Poland, a farmer named Jan Walski was driving his horse-drawn cart when he encountered two aliens (left) in dark uniforms with hoods. He described them as having narrow lips and slanted eyes. They were apparently friendly, even playful, and invited him aboard their ship. There he was carefully examined and offered food which he declined. After he left the craft, it took off horizontally and flew away.

For most of the people who believe they were abducted by aliens, their experiences were both frightening and exciting. Why frightening? Because no one wants to be controlled by another person—or thing. Would you like to be taken from your house or car? Would you like to have examinations and experiments done to you without your permission? How do you think you'd feel?

At the same time, the abductions, if true, offer clues to other peoples and other worlds that we've never known before.

The many similarities in the reports suggest that the aliens seen so far have certain common physical traits: They are short, wear uniforms, and have slanted or strange-looking eyes.

But the reports also raise many questions. Do aliens have languages, or do they communicate strictly by telepathy—thought transference? Many of the victims say no words were actually spoken in their encounters.

Do abductions change according to the country or culture where they occur? Some say the answer is yes. American ufologist Allan Hendry has said, "South Americans produce CE III [Close Encounters of the Third Kind] that are especially vivid; the entities, often more animalistic or 'ugly' than those reported in North America, are reported to behave more aggressively towards South American humans."

Why would they behave differently toward people in different cultures?

We have seen that some aliens are experimental, curious, and ruthless—they do what they want with humans, even if in a gentle way. But there are other reports of encounters that are on a friendlier, more equal basis. These involve contacts, but no abductions. Do extraterrestrials have friendly encounters with certain earth people?

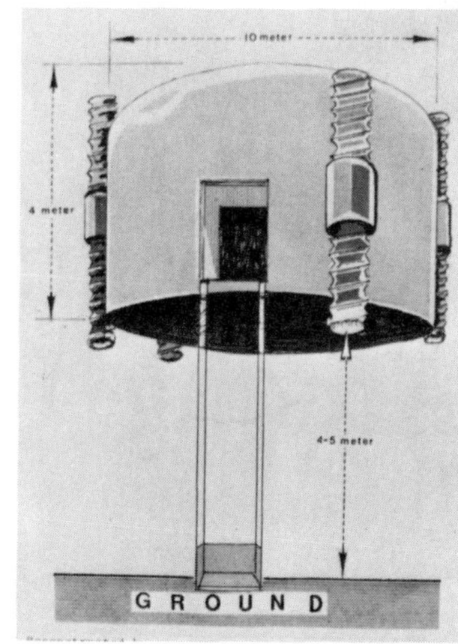

The craft as Jan Walski described it.

Five

Are Extraterrestrials Among Us?

Opposite page: Mt. Auruti stands in the background, giving perspective to one of the spacecraft which visited Eduard Meier regularly. He took an 8mm film of this scene which showed two red lights on the bottom of the ship and a sudden brightening of a red light on the ship's rim.

Are there friendly aliens as well as abductors? Gary Kinder, in his book *Light Years,* weaves a fascinating story of Eduard Meier, a Swiss caretaker who claims to personally have been in contact with an alien race since 1975. In UFO terminology, Meier is called a "contactee," or a person aliens have communicated with on a friendly basis. He also has taken hundreds of photographs of the aliens' ships and recorded the sounds that the "beamships" make.

Meier's aliens call themselves *Pleiadians.* They come from the constellation Pleiades, also known as the Seven Sisters. It is visible in our night sky and it is about five hundred million light-years away.

Semjase

Meier states that he was "telepathically [mentally] contacted by alien beings" and was often directed to go to remote locations to meet the aliens. Meier was especially befriended by an alien woman, Semjase, who apparently spoke to Meier about life in the galaxy and Earth's place in the cosmic scheme of things. She informed him of interstellar travel, life on her home planet Erra, universal law, physics, and the fate of other human races.

Swiss UFO contactee Eduard Meier.

Meier kept a journal of the rendezvous and his conversations with Semjase. In one entry, he recorded these words of Semjase:

> We, too, are still far removed from perfection and have to evolve constantly. When we choose to come in contact with an earth human, we do so because we feel an obligation to the developing universe, and to life which is already existing throughout the universe. We are not missionaries or teachers, but we endeavor to keep order throughout all areas of space. Now and then we begin contacts with inhabitants of different worlds by searching out individuals whom we feel can accept our existence. We then impart information to those contacts but only when their race has developed and begins to think. Then slowly we and others prepare them for . . . truth, that they are not the only thinking beings in the universe.

As word of Meier and his contact spread, people flocked to his house to learn more about the aliens. Meier relayed some historical information regarding the ancient Pleiadians, who apparently are like colonizers of space. According to Meier, the Pleiadians live to be one thousand years old. Semjase herself was a comparatively young 330. Her home planet, Erra, was only slightly smaller than Earth, yet was populated by far fewer people, less than five hundred million. Upon discovering Erra's hospitable but young environment, the Pleiadians had engineered the planet to support life. Today, according to Meier, its landscape looks much like the countryside found on Earth, with hills, grass, trees, and running water.

Contact with Semjase

Semjase told Meier that the Pleiadians long ago had mated with primitive humans. They had created a generation of people who were eventually destroyed by war. Those who survived were our ancestors. As a result, Pleiadians now feel responsible for helping humanity.

Also, Semjase explained the Pleiadians's propulsion system used in starships. It was a system that enabled them to travel faster than the speed of light. They get to earth in only seven hours. "The reason we need seven hours to reach earth is first we must fly far into space before we can convert to hyperspeed. We then come back out of the hyper-space conditions far outside of your solar system, and fly to here once more in a normal drive."

She told Meier that hyperdrive can paralyze—or freeze—time and space. "And only when time and space have ceased to exist are we capable of traveling through distances of light years in a tiny particle of a second."

The Pleiades are a loose cluster of stars in the constellation Taurus. People all over the world have developed myths about this group of stars.

Is This All True?

Can we believe these conversations? Author Gary Kinder says that mythology can at least help us to speculate. He reports that Lee Elders and Tom Welch, two investigators of the Meier case, researched information on the Pleiades and turned up an abundance of references to the constellation in their readings. Throughout the human history of earth, they found that history and mythology have mentioned the Pleiades many times. One of the researchers says of the Pleiades, "They're noted as being the source of knowledge in the rice culture of Asia and in the potato culture of Europe and South America. These societies attributed their knowledge to a series of events in mythological form involving messengers from Pleiades. . . . They're looked at as the center of heaven, and they're looked at as a source of ancestry and wisdom and guidance."

Moreover, Kinder says that the Hopi, an American Indian tribe in the southwest U.S., refer to the Pleiades as *Choo-ho-kan*, or *Home of Our Ancestors.* The Navajos have a similar belief.

Aside from mythology, is there any documented proof concerning Meier's claims? What about the

"Wendelle Stevens examined each print carefully, holding it up to the light and tilting it. In thirty years of collecting and analyzing photographs of UFOs, Meier's photos were the most spectacular he had ever seen."

Author Gary Kinder, *Light Years: An Investigation into the Extraterrestrial Experiences of Eduard Meier*

photographs? Are they genuine?

Although it is not possible to be absolutely certain whether pictures are real without the original negatives, they *could* be the real thing. Dr. Michael Malin, a physics professor at the University of California at Berkeley, helped analyze NASA's photographs of Mars. He has studied some of Meier's photos. Kinder quotes Malin: "I find the photographs themselves credible. They're good photographs. They appear to represent real phenomena. The story that some farmer in Switzerland is on a first-name basis with dozens of aliens who come and visit him. . . . I find that incredible. But I find the photographs more credible. They're reasonable evidence of something. What that something is I don't know."

Kinder says that Neil Davis, owner of a photo lab in San Diego, tested one of the photos—a spaceship 150 feet in the air. He did not discover anything that would point to a fraud.

However, Rudolf Ruegg, one of the town administrators where Meier lived, expressed doubts about Meier's stories. He thought they were "imagined, invented; I think he invented it all."

Martin Sorge, a skeptic who also investigated the case, had this conclusion:

"I saw pictures of a UFO and it really was a model. In the first place I *saw* that it was a model, and in the second place I learned it from his wife."

Meier skeptic Martin Sorge, quoted in *Light Years: An Investigation into the Extraterrestrial Experiences of Eduard Meier*

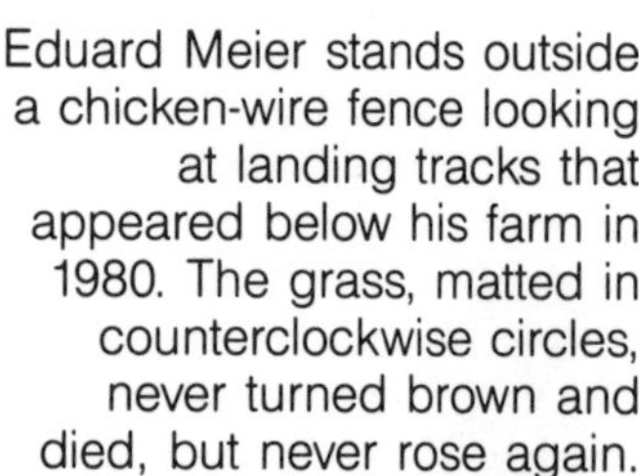

Eduard Meier stands outside a chicken-wire fence looking at landing tracks that appeared below his farm in 1980. The grass, matted in counterclockwise circles, never turned brown and died, but never rose again.

> I am certain he has had these contacts, but not in the way he's telling us. He may receive them in the form of visions, the way mediums [psychics] receive things. He may not even know himself if these visions are real. But for him it is reality. . . .
>
> He is not flying away and he is not meeting with Semjase, but he is able to put himself into a parallel world, and he has his experiences in this parallel world. He fakes the evidence to make people understand his experiences.

Sorge believes Meier is psychic! But apparently Sorge believes that this parallel world is purely a mental one rather than physical.

Gary Kinder suspects that there is more to the story than meets the eye. "After three years of research I have concluded that UFOs exist: Something we cannot explain indeed sails through our skies from time to time."

A jet fighter on maneuvers with the Swiss Air Force flew into the background as Meier took this photo near Schmarduel on April 14, 1976.

Author Ruth Montgomery.

In a startling book, *Aliens Among Us,* well-known psychic and writer Ruth Montgomery tells us that extraterrestrials are already living among us.

Walk-Ins

According to Montgomery, the aliens are here to help prepare and guide humans to a New Age, a time based on love and harmony between peoples. She believes that sometimes with or without permission, the aliens take over and inhabit people's bodies. Apparently this usually occurs when a person has finished his or her life purpose or else simply does not want to live anymore. The alien personality then enters and takes over the body.

How does Montgomery know all this? Because she is a psychic who has "spiritual Guides" who relay information to her through psychic means.

> The so-called space people are in actuality ones like yourselves, who are also space people in the sense that all of us inhabit a universe that is whirling in orbit. When those souls who inhabit other spheres visit the earth they come as humanoids [resembling humans], because otherwise they would be captured or repelled or humiliated by those who would make of them a laughing stock. To understand why they arrive on earth is to explore the plan of universal brotherhood. . . .
>
> Not all space travellers are from any one planet. They come as explorers and observers and intend no harm, although harm sometimes results, inadvertently. They are not of this galaxy, as there is no humanoid type of life on the planets in the same galaxy as earth, although there once was. Those who visit earth at this time are from planets with highly advanced technology and science. They have solved the challenge of space travel through dissolving atoms and reconstituting them in the earth's atmosphere and on other planets.
>
> Space aliens are able to dissolve the atomic structures of their spaceships as well as their bodies

and to reassemble the atoms as they reach earth's outer atmosphere.

Does this sound like Captain Kirk in the television series "Star Trek"? Or do different races of aliens have different technologies?

Semjase said the aliens dematerialize and materialize themselves, they sort of dissolve into nothing and reassemble at their destination; they do not need spaceships. Which version is true? Are both true? We, too, have different means of transportation: cars, trains, buses, jets, and space shuttles for astronauts. Perhaps alien races have different transport for different purposes—spaceships for one kind of journey; dematerialization and materialization for another.

What do Montgomery's Guides say about abductions? They partially confirm Martin Sorge's belief that UFO contact experiences are mental. "They [ab-

"It would seem very difficult, if not impossible, to accept the stories of the contactees."

Author Len Ortzen, *Strange Stories of UFOs*

"It's very easy to denounce the contactees as frauds. . . . Yet fraud does not entirely explain the phenomenon of the contactees."

Author Daniel Cohen, *The World of UFOs*

"Star Trek" Captain Kirk and friends in the transporter room. They were able to move great distances by "beaming," or disassembling and then reassembling themselves at the touch of a few buttons.

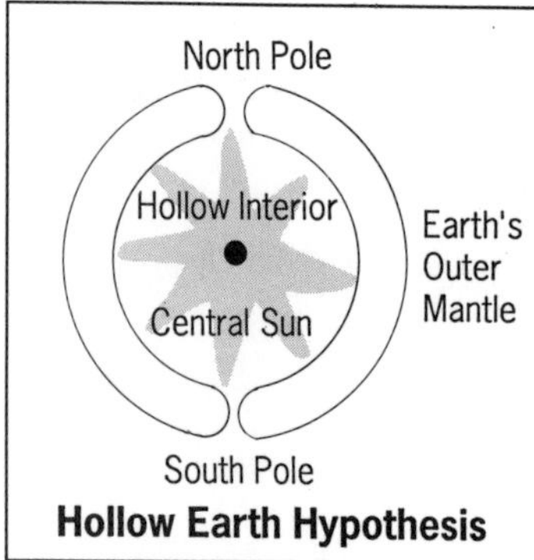

This diagram shows one version of the hollow earth theory. The interior of the earth is supposed to be inhabited by citizens of Atlantis or aliens using the area as a base camp for trips to the surface of the earth.

ductees] regard it later as a brief amnesia, but actually they are experiencing it at another level of consciousness.'' Montgomery asked the Guides if humans were taken aboard UFOs by mental or physical means. They said it happens both ways.

If we believe the Guides, then what they say clears up some of our UFO theories. Montgomery quotes the Guides: ''The extraterrestrials do not have a base in your oceans, and we have previously told you that there is nothing to the hollow-earth theory, or a civilization operating beneath the surface of the earth. The extraterrestrials come and go at will because of their ability to disintegrate solids and reassemble them wherever they wish.''

Why are aliens so interested in human beings? The Guides supply us with one reason. During the time an earthling is in a UFO, the aliens are studying how to live and operate inside that person's body. Imagine a person who has been bedridden for months because of an accident and then has to learn how to walk again. It would be a similar situation for an alien entering a strange body and becoming a ''Walk-In.''

Charlotte King

Montgomery described a Walk-In: Charlotte King, of Sacramento, California, has perplexed geologists and scientists with her uncanny ability to detect coming earthquakes and volcanic eruptions. For example, she accurately predicted the precise dates and times of the Mount St. Helens eruptions in the state of Washington during 1980.

Dr. Frank Yatsu, at the University of Texas School of Medicine, compared King's ability to that of certain animals which seem to ''predict'' earthquakes through their behavior. He said, ''Charlotte may be detecting shifts in the earth's electromagnetic field, which may also affect certain animals and cause them to behave in an unusual manner, a phenomenon long under serious study in Russia and China.''

How did Charlotte acquire such an ability? Perhaps she is not from earth.

In 1976, jobless and separated from her husband on Christmas Day, Charlotte attempted suicide. While she was in the hospital she "became aware that I did not want to die. I knew I had a job to do, that my kids needed me and my marriage could be salvaged." Montgomery says that during Charlotte's stay in the hospital when she was unconscious, the "old" Charlotte left her body and the "new" Charlotte entered. The new personality was a Walk-In from the star Sirius. She was here to warn humans of coming earthquakes and devastating geological shifts in the earth.

A bizzare story? Do Walk-Ins exist? Are aliens here to help humanity, not harm us? Montgomery certainly has given us provocative food for thought.

Charlotte King claims she can accurately predict earthquakes because she hears a low frequency tone before one happens. Is that how she knew that Mount St. Helens would erupt? Is she a walk-in or just an extremely sensitive person?

Epilogue

The Mystery Continues

Throughout history people have sighted UFOs. In this book, we have explored some of their mystery. Yet there are many unanswered questions including the most basic: Do they come from outer space or are they tricks played by nature, imagination, and hoaxes?

Let us keep in mind what retired air force pilot Wendelle Stevens said about them. The UFO phenomenon is "too widespread to be nothing but a mental aberration." Let us keep trying to discover the answers, for the mystery continues.

The photo opposite was taken by Paul Trent on May 11, 1950 when his wife called him to the backyard to witness what appeared to be a flying saucer. Over the years, Trent's photo has been subjected to numerous tests. William Spaulding of Ground Saucer Watch used computer enhancement analysis which he believes proves that the photo is not a fake.

Organizations to Contact

BUFORA (British UFO Research Association)
30 Vermont Rd.
Upper Norwood, London SE19 35R

NUFON (Northern UFO Network)
8 Whitethroat Walk
Birchwood, Cheshire WA3 6PQ

CUFOS (Center for UFO Studies)
PO Box 1621
Lima, Ohio 45802

APRO (Aerial Phenomena Research Organization)
3910 East Kleindale Rd.
Tucson, Arizona 85712

MUFON (Mutual UFO Network)
103 Oldtowne Rd.
Sequin, Texas 78155

About the Author

Michael Arvey is a free-lance writer who has lived all over the U.S. He currently teaches correspondence courses in creative writing. At various times, he has also been a meditation instructor, massage therapist, and poet.

Michael's interest in UFOs comes from his having seen one. He believes that without mysteries such as UFOs, the world would be a dull place.

For Further Exploration

George C. Andrews, *Extra-Terrestrials Among Us*. St. Paul, MN: Llewellyn Publications, 1987.

Daniel Cohen, *The Ancient Visitors*. New York: Doubleday, 1976.

Daniel Cohen, *The World of UFOs*. New York: J.B. Lippincott Company, 1978.

Thomas R. McDonough, *The Search for Extraterrestrial Intelligence*. New York: John Wiley & Sons, 1987.

Len Ortzen, *Strange Stories of UFOs*. New York: Taplinger Publishing Company, 1977.

Margaret Sachs, *The UFO Encyclopedia*. New York: G.P. Putnam's Sons, 1980.

Ronald D. Story, *UFOs and the Limits of Science*. New York: William Morrow and Company, 1981.

Jacques Vallee, *UFOs in Space: Anatomy of a Phenomenon*. New York: Ballantine, 1965.

Additional Bibliography

Isaac Asimov, *Extraterrestrial Civilizations*. New York: Crown Publishers, 1979.

Jacques Bergier, *Extra-Terrestrial Visitations from Prehistoric Times to the Present*. Chicago: Henry Regnery Company, 1973.

Maurice Chatelain, *Our Ancestors Came from Outer Space*. New York: Doubleday, 1978.

James C. Christian, *Extra-Terrestrial Intelligence: The First Encounter.* New York: Prometheus Books, 1976.

Daniel Cohen, *A Close Look at Close Encounters*. New York: Dodd, Mead & Company, 1981.

Erich von Däniken, *Chariots of the Gods?* New York: Bantam Books, 1970.

Erich von Däniken, *Signs of the Gods?* New York: G.P. Putnam's Sons, 1980.

Edward Edelson, *Who Goes There?* New York: Doubleday, 1979.

Sylvia Louise Engdahl, *The Planet-Girded Suns*. New York: Atheneum, 1974.

Randall Fitzgerald, *The Complete Book of Extraterrestrial Encounters*. New York: Collier Books, 1979.

Paris Flammonde, *UFOs Exist!* New York: Ballantine Books, 1976.

Raymond E. Fowler, *The Andreasson Affair.* New York: Bantam Books, 1979.

John G. Fuller, *The Interrupted Journey.* New York: The Dial Press, 1966.

Michael H. Hart and Ben Zuckerman, eds., *Extraterrestrials: Where Are They?* Elmsford, NY: Pergamon Press, 1982.

Richard C. Hoagland, *The Monuments of Mars*. Berkeley, CA: North Atlantic Books, 1987.

Budd Hopkins, *Intruders, The Incredible Visitations at Copley Woods*. New York: Random House, 1987.

J. Allen Hynek, *The UFO Experience: A Scientific Inquiry.* Chicago: Henry Regnery Company, 1972.

Gary Kinder, *Light Years: An Investigation into the Extraterrestrial Experiences of Eduard Meier.* New York: The Atlantic Monthly Press, 1987.

Philip Klass, *UFOs Explained.* New York: Random House, 1974.

Donald H. Menzel, *Flying Saucers.* Cambridge, MA: Harvard University Press, 1953.

Donald H. Menzel and Ernest H. Taves, *The UFO Enigma.* New York: Doubleday, 1977.

Ruth Montgomery, *Aliens Among Us.* New York: G.P. Putnam's Sons, 1985.

James E. Oberg, *UFOs & Outer Space Mysteries.* Norfolk, VA: Donning Publishers, 1982.

Jenny Randles and Peter Warrington, *Science and the UFOs.* New York: Basil Blackwell, Inc., 1985.

Ian Ridpath, *Messages from the Stars.* New York: Harper & Row, 1978.

D. Scott Rogo, *Alien Abductions: True Cases of UFO Kidnappings.* New York: New American Library, 1980.

Carl Sagan, *The Cosmic Connection.* New York: Doubleday, 1978.

Carl Sagan, *Cosmos.* New York: Random House, 1980.

Robert Sheaffer, *The UFO Verdict: Examining the Evidence.* New York: Prometheus Books, 1981.

Brad Steiger, *Project Blue Book.* New York: Ballantine Books, 1976.

Ronald D. Story, *Guardians of the Universe?* New York: St. Martin's Press, 1980.

Whitley Strieber, *Communion: A True Story.* New York: Avon Books, 1987.

Index

Accetta, Joseph S., 71
Andreasson, Becky, 87
Andreasson, Betty, 86-88
Andrews, George C., 8-10, 41, 65
Arnold, Kenneth, 48-50, 61
Asimov, Isaac, 22
Atlantis, 44

black holes, 23, 64

Center for UFO Studies (CUFOS), 77
Chatelain, Maurice, 30-33, 39-40
Close Encounters of the Third Kind, 8, 17
Cohen, Daniel, 41, 50-51, 64, 66-67, 85
Condon Committee, 73, 75-76
Cro-Magnon, 30, 32, 92
crystal skull, 40-41

Darwin, Charles, 14
Däniken, Erich von, 30, 33-37, 39-40
Druffel, Ann, 92

E.T., 8
Enley, George W., 46
evolution, 14
extraterrestrials
  abduction cases, 78, 93, 101-102
    and hypnosis, 84, 86, 87
    and medical examinations, 85, 88, 90
    Antonio Villas-Boas, 89-91
    Betty and Barney Hill, 80-86
    Betty Andreasson, 86-88
  and contactees, 94-103
  and nuclear war, 41, 53-54, 65
  as human ancestors, 20, 30-33, 92, 96
  as walk-ins, 100-103
  communication with, 54, 61, 94-97
    by radio signals, 22, 23-27
  descriptions of, 17-18, 19, 66, 83, 86-88
  evidence of visits, 35-41, 44
  in the Bible, 13, 33-34
  on Mars, 41-46

Fermi, Enrico, 20
flying saucers, 48
  see UFOs
Fontes, Olavo T., 69, 89
Fowler, Raymond, 71, 87
Fuller, John, 80-81, 85-86

Gold, Thomas, 20, 26
Gordon, Flash, 8, 34
Grossinger, Richard, 43, 45, 47

Halt, Charles, 8, 10
Hart, Michael, 21-22
Hendry, Allan, 93
Hewish, Anthony, 24-26
Hill, Betty and Barney, 80-86, 91
Hillsdale College
  and UFOs, 58-59
Hoaglund, Richard C., 42-45
Howard, James, 59
Hynek, J. Allen, 59, 76-77

Incas, 35

Jung, Carl, 64

Keel, John, 65
Kinder, Gary, 94, 97-99
King, Charlotte, 102-103
Klass, Philip, 29, 61-63
Kosok, Paul, 37

Lhullier, Alberto Ruz, 38-40
Lipp, J.E., 54
Little Green Men theory, 25, 70

McDonald, James E., 63
McDonough, Thomas R., 12, 14-16, 20, 25, 26
Malin, Michael, 98
Mannor, Frank, 59

Mantell, Thomas, 50-52
Mars, 42-45
Mayans, 38, 40
Meier, Eduard, 94-99
Menzel, Donald H., 38, 51, 73, 74
Milky Way, 20, 22
Mitchell-Hedges, F.A., 41
Montgomery, Ruth, 100-102

National Aeronautics and Space Administration (NASA), 52, 70
  and *Gemini 7*, 73
  and Mars "face", 43-46
  and *Viking* probes, 42-45
National Center for Atmospheric Research, 21
Nazca lines in Peru, 35-38
Neanderthal, 30, 32, 92
Nott, Julian, 38

Oberg, James E., 73, 85
origin of life, 14-16, 20
Ortzen, Len, 57, 58, 59-60, 73

Palenque carving, 38-40
Pleiades, 94, 96-97
Project Blue Book, 74-77
Project Grudge, 75, 76
Project Sign, 74, 76

Quintanilla, Hector, 77

radio telescopes, 24-29
Ridpath, Ian, 16, 24, 26-28
Rogers, Buck, 8, 34
Rogo, D. Scott, 78, 86, 88, 92
Ruppelt, Edward J., 75

Sachs, Margaret, 55-56, 60-61
Sagan, Carl, 16, 19, 20, 22-23, 33
Scheaffer, Robert, 84
Scully, Frank, 70
Seamans, Robert C., 75-76
Semjase, 96-97, 101
Sigismond, Richard, 16-17
Sorge, Martin, 98-99, 101
space travel, 21-23
"Star Trek", 8, 101
Steiger, Brad, 74
Story, Ronald D., 34, 37, 38-40, 62, 66, 67, 69, 72
Streiber, Whitley, 17-19
Sued, Ibrahim, 67-68

Tassili cave paintings, 40
Taves, Ernest H., 38, 73, 74
Tesla, Nikola, 23-24

UFOs
  air force investigations of, 73-77
  and science, 16-29
  descriptions of, 52-53, 59
  evidence of, 29, 67-69, 70, 71
  explanations for, 64-66
    as hoaxes, 60-61, 62, 70, 72-73
    as natural phenomena, 50-52, 58, 59, 62-63, 71-72
    from other civilizations, 55-56, 64-65
  history of, 11-13, 52
  in the Bible, 13, 33-34
  in the media
    Close Encounters of the Third Kind, 8, 17
    E.T., 8
    War of the Worlds, 42
  photographs of, 61, 72-74, 94, 98
  reports of, 8-10, 48-50, 52-54, 56, 59, 77
    classification of, 54-55

Vallee, Jacques, 11, 52, 54, 77
Verschuur, Gerrit, 27-28
Villas-Boas, Antonio, 89-91

Walker, Walter, 69
War of the Worlds, 42
Washington National Airport and UFOs, 56-58
Wells, H.G., 42
Williams, Dave, 70
Woodman, Jim, 38
Wow signal, 26

Yatsu, Frank, 102

Zamora, Lonnie, 61-62

Picture Credits

Hannah McRoberts/Fortean Picture Library, 9
Jerry Ohlinger's Movie Stills, 10, 46, 101
Mary Evans Picture Library, 11, 34, 53T, 56, 71B, 82, 89
Fortean Picture Library, 12, 66, 70, 91
The Bettmann Archive, 15, 19, 23B, 32T, 35, 51T, 55B, 59
Photograph by J. Kelly Beatty, courtesy *Sky & Telescope* magazine, 17
Amy Johnson, 18
Palomar Observatory Photograph, 21
National Aeronautics and Space Administration, 22B, 25, 27, 43, 45
UPI/Bettmann Newsphotos, 22T, 42, 63, 80, 105
Copyright © Michael Freeman, 23T
Courtesy AT&T Archives, 24
Courtesy Ohio State University Radio Observatory, 26
Courtesy Arecibo Observatory, National Astronomy & Ionosphere Center, 28
Minneapolis Public Library Picture Collection, 31, 39, 73, 79, 90
American Museum of Natural History, Courtesy Department Library Services, (Neg. No. 323737, Photo: Rota), 32B
COMSTOCK, INC./Georg Gerster, 36, 37
Larry Dale Gordon, 38
ICUFON Archives, 40, 51B, 54, 57, 76B, 92, 93
Lowell Observatory Photograph, 44
AP/Wide World Photos, 49, 50T, 67, 68, 74, 76T, 77, 100, 103R
René Dahinden/Fortean Picture Library, 50B
Center for UFO Studies, 52, 58, 61, 75
Shin-ichiro Namiki/Fortean Picture Library, 55T
FATE Magazine/Mary Evans Picture Library, 60
Ann Ronan Picture Library, 62
Fotorama/Fortean Picture Library, 65
Courtesy Raymond Fowler, 71T, 86, 87
From *The Interrupted Journey* by John G. Fuller. New York: Dial Books, 1966, 83, 84, 85
Dennis Stacey/Fortean Picture Library, 88
From the book *LIGHT YEARS*. Copyright © 1987 by Gary Kinder and Intercep. Reproduced here by permission of the Atlantic Monthly Press, 95, 96, 98, 99
Mount Wilson and Las Campanas Observatories, Carnegie Institution of Washington, 97
Mary Ahrndt, 102
U.S. Geological Survey, 103L

001.9 Arvey, Michael
ARV

UFOs

$12.95

DATE			

THE BAKER & TAYLOR CO.